Zimbabwe's origina

The Bulawayo Cookery Book and Household Guide

Mrs. N. H. Chataway

JEPPESTOWN

The Bulawayo Cookery Book and Household Guide.

(Compiled by Mrs. N. H. Chataway.)
In aid of the Building Fund for the New English Church, Bulawayo.

We may do without love,
We may do without books,
But where is the man
Who can do without cooks?

BULAWAYO,
1909.
[*Copyright.*]

BULAWAYO:
PHILPOTT AND COLLINS, PRINTERS, STATIONERS, BOOKBINDERS, ETC.

Published by Jeppestown Press,
10A Scawfell St, London, E2 8NG, United Kingdom.

First published by Philpott & Collins, in aid of the Building Fund
for the New English Church, Bulawayo, Rhodesia, 1909.

Introduction © Copyright David Saffery 2006
Cover design © Copyright Chris Eason 2006

Front cover shows *Granite kopje in early evening, Marabada, Zimbabwe*, by
Kevin Walsh, 2005; www.flickr.com/photos/86624586@N00/.
Reproduced under CCPL:
http://creativecommons.org/licenses/by/2.0/legalcode; *Magistrates and
Staff, Bulawayo Magistrates Court*, c1920, photographer unknown; *8th
Avenue* and *Bulawayo Post Office*, postcards c1930, photographer
unknown. Back cover shows *High Court*, Lobengula Street, Bulawayo,
postcard c1935, photographer unknown.

ISBN: 0-9553936-2-0
ISBN 13: 978-0-9553936-2-4

Introduction

The Bulawayo Cookery Book was Zimbabwe's first cookery book, and the product of a publishing industry that began in 1897—just twelve years before the publication of this book—when the Times Printing Works set up its workshop in Bulawayo, the colonial settlement founded near the ruins of king Lobengula's capital.

This book was originally published to raise funds for the completion of the Anglican church of St. John the Baptist, which was estimated in 1896 to cost £6,000. The list of contributors provides a roll-call of familiar names from the early colonial period of Zimbabwean history: Hester Vintcent, wife of the senior judge and sometime Administrator of Southern Rhodesia, Sir Joseph Vintcent; Colonel Robert 'Boomerang' Gordon, D.S.O., O.B.E., who raised and commanded the Northern Rhodesia Rifles during the First World War; Frances Heyman, later Lady Heyman, wife of a senior officer in the British South Africa Police, who had laid the foundation stone of St John the Baptist; Margaret Issels, who determinedly carted one of the first pianos into Zimbabwe by ox-waggon in 1894; and Frances Carbutt, whose husband, Colonel Clive Carbutt, later became Chief Native Commissioner.

Louise Chataway, who compiled this volume, was born in Dublin in 1865. As a young woman she came to London, where she lodged in a Bloomsbury boarding house with her friend Annie, who worked alongside her in a savings bank. One of their fellow lodgers was a nineteen-year-old merchant's clerk called Norman Chataway; Louise and Norman fell in love, were married in 1895, and emigrated to Rhodesia, where Norman Chataway took a job with the British South Africa Company. They spent the rest of their lives in Africa: Norman Chataway died in January 1935, and Louise died shortly afterwards.

As a snapshot of Edwardian cookery, Louise Chataway's book illuminates the history of colonial settlement in southern and central Africa. The most obvious aspect of this book is the preponderance of comfortable, middle-class British family dishes: stuffed shoulder of mutton, hot pot, Victoria sandwich, walnut toffee. And yet, look more closely at the composition of the recipes and the unmistakeable flavours of southern Africa become evident. The recipe of Mrs. Glanville (whose husband was the Editor of the *Bulawayo Chronicle*) for 'Babotee' ("A nice way of doing up cold meat") is better known as the Cape dish *bobotie*, while Mrs. Crake's tomato and mutton stew, with its red chilli and sugar, is in fact a rich, aromatic tomato bredie—another dish straight from the Cape Muslim tradition. Later in the book, Miss Fynn's recipes for *naartje* (clementine) and green fig *konfyt*, a luscious, whole-fruit conserve, are identical to traditional preserving recipes of the Afrikaans community still used in southern Africa.

The domestic economics of early colonial life also informed the recipes that Mrs. Chataway collected. With limited supplies of fresh fish available in southern Africa until the advent of a comprehensive and reliable railway network, most of the fish recipes are designed for use with tinned fish. The inclusion of recipes (such as Mrs Myburgh's Auntie's Pudding) which need no eggs, may be readily understood when looking at the letters of contemporary writers such as Sheila Macdonald, who wrote to her mother in 1907 that eggs cost five shillings for a dozen—a staggering £15 per dozen in 2006 terms.

Enjoy the recipes and original advertisements in this charming and evocative book.

Contents

- Drapery. -

Walter Edwards

Fife Street.

❀❀❀

THE HOUSE FOR PARIS
AND
CONTINENTAL FASHIONS

❀❀❀

NOVELTIES CONTINUALLY ARRIVING.

❀❀❀

LADIES' TRIMMED MILLINERY AND
BLOUSES A SPECIALITY.

❀❀❀

P.O. BOX 133.   BULAWAYO.

Hors d'oeuvres.

A Simple *Hors d'Oeuvre.*
Miss Hodges.
Cut some thin slices of bread and stamp out with a round cutter about the size of a five shilling piece. Toast and then dip into hot butter; cover with grated yolk of hard-boiled egg, and lay on each one a small round boneless anchovy. Put a caper in the centre of each anchovy, dust with paprika or cayenne, and squeeze a drop of lemon juice over. Put in ice chest until wanted.

Bulawayo Savoury.
Mrs. Norman Chataway.
Stamp out some rounds of white bread and butter, spread these with white mayonnaise (made with egg white, lemon juice and cream, instead of oil, vinegar and egg yolk) and cover with shredded chicken and ham or tongue, sprinkle over this minced olives, and a tiny pinch of paprika.

Tomato and Cheese.
Mrs. Selmes.
Stamp out some small rounds of bread and butter, spread them with any savoury paste, anchovy, bloater, sardine, &c. Peel one or two tomatoes carefully by dipping them for a few minutes in boiling water, cut them into even slices, lay one slice on each round of bread and sprinkle the top with grated cheese.

20

Soups.

Browning to Colour Soups and Gravies

Mrs. P. Fletcher.

Put one cup of sugar dry into a saucepan. Stand it over a hot fire and stir continually until it is reduced to a dark-brown liquid. When it begins to burn and smoke add hastily two cups of boiling water, stir and cook until a thin syrup-like mixture is formed. It must not be too thick. Bottle and it is ready for use and will keep any length of time. 1 find it indispensable in the kitchen.

Celery Soup.

Mrs. Geo. Johnson.

Cut a head of celery into small pieces and boil till tender in 3 pints of water, with salt, a small onion and a sprig of parsley. When cold rub through a sieve. Put a tablespoon of butter in a pan, and add a tablespoon of flour. Mix slowly and stir in a pint of hot milk. Add celery stock and cool: till creamy and smooth. Serve with fried bread.

Children's Favourite Soup.

A Danish Recipe.

To a quart of cold water put 1 lb. of fresh strawberries or raspberries (or ½ lb. of jam of either of these if the fresh fruit is unobtainable) and 1 ½ oz. of bread. Let all boil gently for half-an-hour, then pass through a sieve, and return to the pan. Add 4 oz. of sugar (if jam is used, less or no sugar will be needed) one glass white wine, and one teaspoon of cornflour dissolved in a little water, and stir the soup until it boils. Lastly, stir in half a gill of cream off the fire (this may be omitted) and pour over some croutons of bread fried in butter, and sprinkled with castor sugar.

MATABELE LAUNDRY

Economical Brown Soup.

Miss Hodges.

Take two good-sized onions, peel and cut in rings. Put into an iron saucepan about 2 oz. butter or good dripping, and when melted, put in the onions, cover closely and cook for one hour. Then add 2 carrots and 1 large tomato cut up and a quart or more of water, also 2 slices of toast or stale crusts of bread, and, if possible, any bones or scraps of cold meat left from a joint. Put saucepan at back of stove and let it simmer all day, then about half-an-hour before dinner rub all through a sieve, season well with salt and pepper and return to saucepan to re-heat.

Milk Soup.

Mrs. R. M. Townsend.

1 breakfast cup of milk.
3 breakfast cups of water.
1 tablespoonful of butter
1 large onion or potato sliced
Salt and pepper to taste.
Put on all together and boil slowly for an hour or little longer. Strain and serve with a little parsley finely chopped. Is very nice without the parsley.

Julienne Soup.

Mrs. Norman Chataway.

Required some or all of the following vegetables; Carrots, turnips, onions, spring onions, celery, green peas, French beans, lettuce, asparagus points, etc. Butter, salt, sugar, pepper and some clear stock.

Cut the vegetables after cleaning into shreds as thick as a match and about an inch in length (the quantity of stock required will be about six times the measure of the vegetables when cut up). For each ½ pint of vegetables allow an ounce of butter, add a

little sugar and sweat the vegetables in this from 10 to 20 minutes, shaking often, but keeping the lid always tightly closed. Then add the stock, and simmer for an hour very gently.

Mulligatawny Soup.

Mrs. Vintcent.

4 quarts water
6 sheep's trotters
2 onions
4 cloves
4 peppercorns
2 tablespoons curry powder
1 dessert spoon sugar
2 slices of bacon
Salt and pepper to taste
1 dessert spoon vinegar.

Boil the bacon and trotters in the water till tender, remove all the bones, then leave to get cold and remove all fat. Replace on fire and boil. Fry the onions brown in a little butter or fat, mix the curry powder to a paste with a little water, add to the onions. Then add this to the stock, stirring well, also adding all the other ingredients and boil for 4 hours; add a little boiled rice. The trotters to be cut up and served in the soup.

Pea Flour Soup.

Mrs. Vintcent.

Broth that bones and vegetables have been boiled in may be used for this soup. If not too salt, the water in which salt beef has been boiled will answer the purpose. Mix 3 tablespoons of pea flour in enough cold stock to form a smooth paste. Pour 1 quart of boiling stock over the paste, stirring briskly all the time. Put all in a saucepan and season with salt and pepper, and ¼ egg spoon of dried mint, ¼ egg spoon of sugar and the same of mustard. Serve with small dice or croutons of toast.

We take the Cake

FOR

Quality and Price

IN

General Household Drapery.

Morum Bros.,

(Rhodesia Mail Order House),

P.O. Box 160,   BULAWAYO.

Telegrams: "MORUM BROS."

Potato Soup.

Mrs. Crake.

1 oz. butter
2 onions
1 quart water
½ pint milk
Celery
1 tablespoon tapioca
Pepper and salt
1 lb. potatoes.

Melt butter and add potatoes, cut in slices, leave on for 5 minutes, don't allow to colour, add onions and celery. Another 5 minutes, then add water, let boil till vegetables are tender, rub through sieve and return to saucepan with milk and tapioca, and boil till tapioca is clear. A white soup is better made in a steel saucepan.

Vegetable Marrow Soup.

Mrs. Norman Chataway.

Peel and cut up a large vegetable marrow and one onion, and simmer gently in enough water to cover until they are quite soft and can be rubbed through a sieve. Return the pulp to a saucepan with a quart of milk, 2 oz. of butter, pepper, salt, and a grate of nutmeg, and let the whole come to the boil. Serve with croutons of fried bread handed round separately.

Why send away for your Clothing, when you can get the Best Cut Garments made locally and PROPERLY FITTED ON?

Why not spend your money where you make it and support local industries?

J. BANET,

Tailor and Habit Maker,

EIGHTH AVENUE.

P.O. Box 18.

CAIE,

The Practical Watchmaker and Jeweller,

Has opened his

NEW PREMISES

Next door to the old shop, with a

Brilliant Display of New Goods,

✿✿✿

Repairs of all kinds executed on the premises by First-class Workmen.

——ENGRAVING.——

Fish.

A Continental Method of Frying Fish.
Mrs. Selmes.

Wash dry and trim the fish, filleting if desired. Put a few tablespoons of flour on a paper; mix with this a good seasoning of salt and pepper. Pour some milk into a deep dish, draw the fish through the milk, then draw it through the seasoned flour. Again dip it in the milk and lastly again in the flour. Fry at once in a pan of boiling fat. Serve very hot with cut lemon.

Fat is boiling when it is perfectly still and a blue smoke arises from it.

Fish Cream with Shrimps.
Mrs. R. H. Myburgh.

Pass 9 oz. of raw white fish (or any tinned white fish) through mincer and put aside until required. Melt 1 oz. butter and stir in 2 oz. flour. When it is smoothly mixed, add a ¼ pint of milk in which the bones (if any) have been simmered, with a slice of onion, a clove, a thin strip lemon peel, four whole peppercorns and a little salt; stir all the time till sufficiently thickened to leave sides of saucepan; turn on a plate to cool. Pound the minced fish and add the paste when cool, and, lastly, 2 eggs, 1 at a time. Season well and pass through a wire sieve. Whip a ¼ pint of cream, add to the fish, then rather more than half-fill a border mould, which has been brushed over with butter. Cover the cream with buttered paper and steam gently for three-quarters of an hour, when it should be firm to the touch. Turn it carefully from mould, brush over on outside with white sauce, sprinkle with parsley, and fill centre with shrimp sauce tinted pale pink.

— Sweets. —

HOW TO MAKE THEM.

PUT something on your head, something on your feet (in addition, of course, to other apparel) and £1 in your pocket. Walk down or up Main St., Bulawayo, until you arrive at the Albany Tea Rooms, enter, demand of Miss O'Connell how to make sweets. You will not be told but you will be sold—some.

As it is not considered good manners to remove anything hurriedly from your mouth in a room unless special arrangements are made, go outside, stand on the curb and taste. Take time to consider and form no hasty judgment. If the swelling subsides, remove the bandage and wash well in warm water, and— Sorry! I was thinking of an ointment. I should have said: "If you feel allright so far, be duly thankful. If not, take an antidote in the shape of another box. Really, they will do you no physical damage."

There's a purple kind with blue spots and red insides which look like a remedy for rats, but are positively comforting. By the way, of course, you wish to know how to *make* sweets.

Well, it is no easy job to "make" one of Miss O'Connell's sweets! But if you can escape the eagle-eye of Miss N—— "make" hurriedly, then whistle— if you can—to show your innocence. If too succulent to whistle, leave the premises nonchalantly. Miss O'Connell's sweets remind me of Fuller's Buzzards and the toffee I used to make at school all combined. Higher recommendation I cannot give them.

Fish Mould.

Mrs. Winslow.

1 ½ lbs. white fish boiled.

1 oz. butter.

½ teacup bread crumbs.

1 egg.

¾ teacup of milk, salt, pepper

2 teaspoons anchovy sauce

1 teaspoon parsley.

Take the skin off the fish and pass through a mincer. Put in a basin and add bread crumbs, parsley and seasoning, melted butter, milk, and eggs well-beaten. Put in a buttered mould, cover with buttered paper, and steam for three-quarters of an hour. Serve with sauce.

Halibut Pie.

Mrs. Vintcent.

1 tin halibut

¼ onion chopped up fine

¼ lb. bread crumbs

1 teaspoon chopped parsley

Juice of half a lemon

1 egg

1 tablespoon milk

Small piece of butter

Turn the halibut on to a large plate, break up with a fork. Mix in the bread crumbs, lemon juice, parsley and onion, put into a pie dish. Beat the milk and egg together, pour over the top and put the butter on in very small pieces. Bake in moderate oven till a nice brown.

Creamed Lobster.

Mrs. N. Chataway.

Open a tin of lobster, drain, and pick to pieces with two

Geo. CARROL,

(Late CUTHBERT & COY.)

𝔅oot and 𝔖hoe 𝔐erchant,

ABERCORN STREET, BULAWAYO,

FOR

LADIES BOOTS AND SHOES

IN

"LOTUS," "BECTIVE," "ARIEL" and "LIGHTFOOT" Brands

The Best of British-Made Footwear.

A Large and Varied Stock of Children's goods to select from, in White, Black or Tan Leathers.

"C KING" SCHOOL BOOTS FOR BOYS, A SPECIALITY.

Gents' Boots and Shoes in Latest Styles, Excellent Quality and Guaranteed Workmanship.

Country Orders receive prompt personal attention. Five per cent. discount allowed on all purchases over 20/-

P.O. Box 312.   **Telegrams "CARROLS."**

forks. Boil 2 eggs hard, shell and chop fine. Put into a saucepan 2 tablespoons butter and when melted, stir in 2 tablespoons flour, when smooth add half-teaspoon grated onion, a pinch of nutmeg, half-teaspoon lemon juice, a good dash of paprika and salt and a pinch of black pepper. Cook smooth and add one-and-a-half pints of milk, stirring all the time until the whole is a rich, creamy sauce, then add the lobster and hard-boiled egg ; turn into a baking dish, cover with bread crumbs and bits of butter, and bake a nice brown on top. Serve hot.

Lobster Rissoles.

Mrs. Nanson.

Take a tin of Lazenby's lobster, put the meat through a fine mincer. Put 1 oz. of butter into a saucepan and, when it is melted, add 1 oz. of flour, stirring it gradually into the butter until a smooth paste is formed: then pour in a quarter-of-a-pint of milk, and continue to stir rapidly until the sauce has boiled and thickened. When this takes place, draw the pan to the side of the stove and add a teaspoon of anchovy essence, a very little salt, some cayenne white pepper, nutmeg, and a few drops of carmine. Then add the minced lobster and, when it is mixed thoroughly with sauce, spread it out on a flat dish. As soon as the lobster mixture is quite cold, take a small quantity at a time and roll it into a medium-sized ball, on a floured board, then mould it quickly between the hands until it is the shape of a cone. When all the mixture has been used, dip the rissoles into beaten egg, then cover them thickly with bread crumbs and fry in deep boiling fat until they are a golden brown, drain on paper and serve neatly arranged and garnished with fried parsley.

Salmon Loaf.

Miss Hodges.

2 tablespoons melted butter
2 eggs well beaten
½ cup fresh bread crumbs
1 tin salmon
Salt, pepper, cayenne or paprika
1 tablespoon chopped parsley.

Mix all these together and steam for one hour in a greased
pound baking powder or cocoa tin. Turn out and serve hot or
cold. It cold, cut into round slices, place a thin slice of lemon on
each slice and serve on a bed of lettuce. If hot, serve whole with
Hollandaise sauce as follows: beat together 2 eggs, 4 tablespoons
tepid water, half-teaspoon salt, a dash of cayenne, and 1
tablespoon of butter cut into bits. Stir over boiling water until the
mixture begins to thicken, then drop in a second tablespoon of
butter, also cut into bits. When as thick as custard, take off, add a
tablespoon of lemon juice and serve either separately or poured
over the loaf.

Tinned Oyster Pie.

An American Recipe.

Make some good short paste, line a deep dish and fill with
uncooked rice or pieces of bread to keep the pastry in shape. A
little before the crust is quite cooked, remove the filling and
return to oven to brown the inside. Meantime open a tin of
oysters, drain and use the liquor with a little cream to make a
good white sauce, flavour well with paprika, salt if necessary,
and pepper, and a dash of nutmeg, take off the fire and, when a
little cool, add the beaten yolks of two eggs, return to the fire
and stir until thick, add the oysters, stirring for a minute or two,
and turn this mixture into the pastry case. Serve cold with
whipped cream; lightly piled over the top.

Entrees.

Brains Au Gratin.

Mrs. R. H. Myburgh.

Parboil brains, cut into slices, toss them in good white sauce, mix in a little grated cheese, cayenne and salt, put in small paper or china cases, strew fried crumbs over, and a little cheese. Bake for 5 minutes and serve hot for entree or savoury.

Creamed Chicken.

Major R. Gordon, D.S.O.

Here is an old colonial recipe for creamed chicken which is delicious: cut up a small cooked chicken into even bits. If you have more than you will need reject part of the dark meat and use more white. Make a cup of rich white sauce, and season well. Put the chicken into this and heat it. Then all the beaten yolk of 2 eggs and stir till smooth, and last put in 2 hard-boiled eggs chopped not too finely. Serve very hot.

Chicken Rolls.

Mrs. R. H. Myburgh.

Bone a chicken, opening it from the back. Trim to an even square; use trimmings to make a forcemeat, with bread crumbs, parsley, chopped bacon, &c.; spread lightly over chicken, roll up to an even roll, sew up or tie in a cloth. Stew very gently in stock or milk till tender. Keep hot. Then cut in rounds about half-an-inch thick and dip each piece in hot white, or brown, or tomato sauce, and serve round green peas or mashed potatoes.

N.B. The same is excellent cold, with a mayonnaise sauce, and salad in centre, or dipped in aspic jelly, and served round salad.

Curried Puffs.

Mrs. Heyman.

Make a good curry sauce, adding some finely chopped meat; make some pastry, cut into squares and fill with the curry mixture, fold over, and bake, and serve very hot as an entrée.

Jugged Beef Steak (Very good).

Mrs. R. H. Myburgh.

Cut some steak into long thin pieces and roll them round. Take a deep stone jar or casserole dish; in this put the rolls one above the other. Add one large onion, one glass of port wine, pepper, salt and few peppercorns. No water to be used. Cover closely, put the jar into a saucepan with boiling water, and steam for four or five hours till tender. All beef stewed in this way is tender and digestible.

A Hot Weather Entree.

Mrs. Norman Chataway.

Peel and mince one onion, fry in hot butter and drain. Add the pulp of a small tomato, a teaspoon of mulligatawny paste, a gill of milk in which a small teaspoon of Bovril has been dissolved, a teaspoon of chutney, salt, pepper, and a pinch of cayenne, nutmeg, and grated lemon peel, and cook all well together. Then pass through a hair sieve and stir in the yolks and whites of two hard-boiled eggs and 6 oz. of cooked white meat or fowl, all of which have been passed through a mincer. Whip a gill of cream stiffly and mix it lightly in, then fill some little paper cases, and sprinkle some chopped chillies, pistachios, or olives on the top of each. Set in the ice chest until just before serving.

A Good Luncheon Mould (or Entrée).

Mrs. R. H. Myburgh

4 oz. macaroni boiled in milk. Shred in a little butter. When cold, mix in two eggs well-beaten, pepper, salt and little nutmeg, a slice of cold meat minced fine with a little ham or lean bacon.

IMPORTANT
MUSICAL ANNOUNCEMENT.

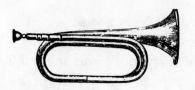

LAURENCE & COPE

PIANOFORTE MAKERS,

MUSIC AND MUSICAL INSTRUMENT DEALERS,

Have removed to

More Extensive Premises,

ABERCORN STREET,

Opposite SCOTCH STORES.

All Goods Imported Direct from
the Manufacturers.

Butter a mould, put in mixture and steam for an hour. Serve with any good gravy or tomato sauce poured over.

Wakefield Steak.

(To make a steak tender).

Mrs. Selmes.

Cut a rump steak 2 inches thick, score it on either side, and lay it in a deep dish in the following mixture for six hours :

1 teaspoon salt
1 teaspoon sugar
1 teaspoon pepper
2 tablespoons vinegar
¼ tablespoon mushroom ketchup

Dredge the steak with a little flour and broil over a clear fire. Warm the mixture and pour over it. Or the steak may be baked in the mixture.

To Ensure
Success -

With the Recipes in
this Book, you will
BE well ADVISED
to purchase your - -
Cooking and Pantry
Stores at - - - -

Haddon & Sly's.

They Stock Everything that
is worth Stocking.

Joints, etc.

Hints on Boiling Meat.

If meat is put into cold water and brought slowly up to boiling point, the meat loses colour and flavour and the soup gains in proportion, therefore, if a good, well-flavoured, boiled joint is required, there must be no idea of making soup from it as well. On the other hand, if put into boiling water and allowed to boil too quickly, it is tough and hard to a degree. The best results are obtained by putting the joint into boiling water and, after a few minutes only, drawing the saucepan to one side of the fire and thereafter allowing it to gently simmer until done. In this way the meat is both tender and well flavoured.

Beef Roll.

Mrs. Puzey.

Take 1½ lbs. of steak and make ¼ lb. veal stuffing and roll up in the middle of steak. Place this into a deep pie dish and pour boiling water over it till the dish is half full. Cover tightly with another dish and bake for 2 hours. When cooked thicken the gravy and serve very hot.

Forcemeat for above.

2 oz. of ham or lean bacon
6 oz. bread crumbs
¼ lb. Suet
2 eggs
1 teaspoon minced parsley
Rind of ½ lemon
1 teaspoon sweet herbs
Salt, cayenne and mace

Mince the bacon, suet, lemon peel, and herbs very finely; add the seasoning to taste and mix with the bread crumbs. Beat the eggs

well and mix into the dry ingredients and the forcemeat is ready for use.

Breast of Lamb and Peas.

Place a breast of lamb in a stew pan with a little water, two or three onions, a carrot, a few pieces of celery, pepper, salt and a sprinkling of parsley and sweet herbs, and cook slowly. Then pull out the bones, and put the breast between two dishes with a heavy weight on top until cold. Cut into small cutlets, egg and breadcrumb them and fry a nice brown, dishing them round a centre mound of peas.

Shoulder of Mutton Stuffed.

Miss Hodges.
Carefully remove the blade from a shoulder and fill the space with a mixture made of:
1 cup bread crumbs
Juice of 1 lemon
2 tablespoons butter
1 teaspoon salt
1 tablespoon chopped parsley
¼ teaspoon pepper
½ tin of oysters, drained from the liquor
1 egg
Sew up the opening and roast in the oven with a little water in the pan, basting frequently. Allow 15 minutes to the lb. Serve with the gravy from the pan after the grease is poured off.

Chicken Casserole.

The thoroughly equipped kitchen of to-day contains at least one good casserole. Into this put a 2 lb chicken, whole but neatly trussed. Sprinkle salt and pepper inside the chicken, and spread the breast thickly with butter. Put on the cover and place in a hot oven for fifteen minutes. Then remove the cover and add three

Bulawayo
Laundry,-

or four shallots, put a handful of breadcrumbs over the chicken, pour around it two cups of milk, and add a little cayenne. Cover the casserole and return it to the oven for another 15 minutes, then remove the cover and let the chicken brown for 10 or 15 minutes. Send to the table in the casserole.

Southern Way of Cooking Ham.

The following recipe for cooking a ham is a time-honoured one, having been used by three generations in one family: soak a ham overnight. Next morning put it in a boiler with enough cold water to cover it, add 1 pint of vinegar, 1½ pints of brown sugar, 1 doz. cloves. Let the ham simmer for three hours then place in a shallow pan (skin side up) with some of the liquor in which it has boiled, and let it bake for two hours. When done remove the skin. Then make a dressing of 1 well-beaten egg, 2 teaspoons of sugar, 1 teaspoon of dry mustard, and half a teaspoon of celery seed. Spread this over the top of the ham, then sprinkle with fine breadcrumbs, and return to the oven to brown.

Beef Neapolitaine.

Mrs. Norman Chataway.

Take a 4 or 5 lb. piece of round of beef, make several slits in it, and insert in each a strip of bacon rolled in powdered sweet herbs and pepper. Lay in a pot lined with chopped bacon, onion, parsley and a sprinkling of sweet herbs. Put over a hot fire until browned, turning frequently, then moisten with 1 pint strained tomato juice and 1 cup stock, add 1 small teaspoon salt, cover and simmer slowly for 2½ hours or until the meat is tender. Serve surrounded by boiled macaroni and pour over the gravy.

Steamed Beef.

A good way of cooking tough meat.

Take the bone from a joint of beef and fill the space with veal stuffing, or any kind preferred. Put the meat on a soup-plate,

and set it in a large saucepan on the top of a weight, or an iron stand or anything that will raise it a few inches above the bottom of the saucepan. Then pour in hot water to create steam. On the top of the meat put some slices of Spanish onion and a few oz. of bacon cut in strips, and just moisten it with a teaspoon of vinegar mixed with a teaspoon or so of stock. Cover closely and cook until the meat is done, about 4 hours for a joint of say 4 lbs. The water should boil steadily the whole time, and, of course, must not be allowed to get into the plate or dish on which the meat is resting. Serve with any nice sauce or gravy, with the liquor from the plate added to it, and, if liked, some dumplings may be made and slipped into the boiling water to cook towards the end of the time.

Puddings and Sweets.

Handy Measures.

Mrs. P. G. Hunt.

The following table will serve as a guide on
ordinary occasions:

2 teaspoons	equal to	1 dessert spoon
2 dessert spoons	"	1 tablespoon
6 tablespoons	"	1 small teacup
1 small teacup	"	1 gill
1 small breakfast cup	"	½ pint
1 oz. dry substance	"	1 tablespoon
1 oz. butter or dripping	"	1 dessert spoon
¼ lb. flour	"	1 teacup
½ lb. flour	"	1 breakfast cup
A teaspoon	holds	a drachm
A tablespoon	"	½ oz
A teacup	"	5 oz.

1 pint is equivalent to 1 lb.
A drop is a minim

Apple Batter Pudding.

Miss B. L. Fynn.

Make a batter with three eggs, cup of flour and cup of milk,
adding a pinch of salt. Peel, core and slice thinly six apples; mix
with the batter and put in a greased mould and steam for three
hours. Serve with custard sauce.

Apple Fool.

Mrs. Nash.

Take about ¼ lb. of dried apple rings, well wash soak in cold
water all night and boil up in same water next morning for about
¾ hour with sugar. Add lemon essence, flavouring to taste. Put

51

through strainer, and mix the pulp with ½ pint of custard made with custard powder.

Apple Mould.

Miss Henderson.
1 lb. apples
1 lemon
3 oz. lump sugar
1 oz. gelatine
½ teaspoon cochineal
Peel and core the apples, cut in pieces and put in a stew pan with the sugar and ½ pint of water, the grated rind and a piece of the lemon. Stew till tender. Dissolve the gelatine in half a gill of cold water. Rub the stewed apple through a sieve, and stir in the melted gelatine. Pour into a mould and stand till set. Serve with whipped cream or custard.

Auntie's Pudding. (No eggs).

Mrs. R. H. Myburgh.
5 tablespoons of raspberry or any sour jam
5 tablespoons suet
12 tablespoons flour
5 tablespoons milk
¼ tablespoon C. of soda
Mix rapidly and cook at once in covered mould. It should swell to twice its size. Steam 2½ hours. 1 tablespoon lemon juice and 1 of treacle does as substitute for jam. This size makes a large pudding.

Banana Cream.

Mrs. Heyman.
Slice some bananas, put a layer in a dish, spread lightly with strawberry jam, bananas again, and repeat until you have a sufficient quantity, also adding chopped pineapple and a little whisky. Cover it with whipped cream and garnish with cherries, angelica and pistachio kernels.

Banana Trifle.

Mrs. J. Macdonald.

Slice half-a-dozen bananas into small bits, then beat up the yolks of 3 eggs, make this into a custard with milk and essence of lemon, pour it when cooked over bananas, then beat up whites of eggs well and put on top with red currant jelly intermixed.

Baked Swiss Pudding.

Mrs. J. Macdonald.

1 lb. apples
¼ lb. bread crumbs
2 oz. suet
3 oz. sugar
A little water and a small piece of butter

Prepare bread crumbs, chop suet, mix all with sugar, cook apples after slicing, put layer of mixture at bottom of greased pie-dish, then layer of apples, then rest of mixture on top; also small pieces butter. Bake in quick oven for half-an-hour.

Boiled Pudding.

Mrs. Clement Dixon.

1 teacup flour
½ teacup sugar
½ teacup milk
1 tablespoon butter
1 teaspoon baking powder

Cream the butter and sugar. Add egg, then milk, then flour and flavouring (some ginger, essence, or a little jam) or put 1 tablespoon of jam on top of mould, and serve with sauce. Boil 2 hours.

Grand
Format
size
6d.
per pkt.
10.

Grand
Format
size
6d.
per pkt.
10.

Save your Cartoon Fronts and secure
a Beautiful Library.

12
for
3d.

12
for
3d.

" Exceed the Speed Limit " for Value.

Brown Pudding.

Mrs. Franklin White.

Two eggs, their weight in flour or butter, the weight of one in sugar. Beat butter to a cream with sugar, add eggs well beaten, stir in flour, then 2 tablespoons of jam or jelly. Before putting the pudding in the mould stir in half a teaspoon of carbonate of soda, boil or steam 1½ hours. Allow plenty of room for the pudding to rise in mould. Golden syrup may be used in place of jam.

Caramel Junket.

Mrs. Byers.

1 pint milk
1 teaspoon rennet
3 tablespoons sugar
Vanilla essence

Put the sugar (granulated is best) into a small frying pan with just enough water to melt it. Stir until sugar is no longer visible, then let it cook without stirring until the syrup becomes a dark brown. Then pour in a few tablespoons of the milk and allow it to cook until strongly flavoured and sweetened by the caramel. Add the flavoured milk to the remainder of the cold milk, then the rennet, flavoured with vanilla, and pour into custard glasses or a glass dish.

Chocolate Junket.

Mrs. Byers.

To make a pint, grate about 2 tablespoons of good unsweetened chocolate, melt it in a little milk, cooking until it is a smooth paste. Sweeten the remainder of the pint of milk, and stir in the chocolate paste which will probably make the milk sufficiently warm for junket. If not, heat a little more. Add the rennet and pour at once into the dish in which it is to be served. Whip a gill of cream, sweeten and flavour with a little vanilla and heap in the centre of the junket, or if served in glasses put a spoonful on each glass.

Egg Jelly.

Mrs. Clarkson Fletcher.

2 oz. isinglass

¼ lb. white sugar

¼ pint water

2 eggs

The rind of 1 lemon

½ pint sherry

Juice of ¼ lemon

1 tablespoon brandy

Grate the lemon rind. Separate whites from the yolks of eggs. Melt the isinglass with the sugar and water, and just boil them. Pour into a basin with all the other ingredients except the whites of the eggs. Whisk until nearly set. Then add the whites beaten to a stiff froth and whisk till jellied. Serve in a rough pile in a glass dish.

Fairy Pudding.

Miss Hendrie.

1 breakfast cup of water

1 lemon

½ teacup of sugar

2 whites of eggs

1 tablespoon cornflour

Put water, juice of the lemon and rind, and sugar on to boil for a minute or two. Mix cornflour with a little water. Put it into the other mixture after taking out the rind. Boil 5 minutes. Beat the whites of eggs, stir in quickly and then pour into a mould.

Fat Rascals.

Mrs. Tonge.

Make sufficient puff paste in the ordinary way, sprinkle in about a teaspoon of castor sugar and also a little salt; scatter some currants in while making. Cut into the desired size pieces before baking; brush over with yolk of egg, place on baking sheet in a quick oven, watch while baking and when it has risen move to a cooler part of the oven and finish.

Fig Pudding.

Mrs. Murray.

¼ lb. dried figs, or dates
2 oz. flour
3 oz. suet
¼ salt spoon nutmeg
2 oz. bread crumbs
1 egg
2 tablespoons milk

Finely chop the figs, add the flour and suet well rubbed together, the bread-crumbs, sugar and nutmeg and mix all well together. Beat the egg and milk together and add to the other ingredients. Turn into a well-greased basin or mould, cover with a buttered paper and steam for six hours.

Five Minutes Pudding.

Mrs. Sly.

2 oz. flour
1½ oz. sugar
2 eggs
1 teaspoon baking powder;
Raspberry jam; flavouring

Put the flour and sugar into a basin, make a hole in the flour, break in the eggs, beat well; add flavouring and baking powder, pour at once into a tin lined with greased paper, and bake in a

J. Wightman

Has on Hand—

Large Stocks of Sanderson's

Colonial Harness & Saddlery

also Boots and Shoes - - -

guaranteed all Leather. - -

P.O. Box 12.
Telephone 129.   Market Square.

hot oven about 5 minutes. Try with a skewer. Turn on to a sugared board. Spread jam on quickly and roll up at once. Sift sugar over.

Fruit Salad.

Mrs. Ll. Webb.

Select 6 nice oranges, taking the inside out and mixing with the ordinary fruits used for fruit salad. Put back in the shells of the oranges, keeping the tops to form the whole orange again. Tie each from underneath with ribbons to match table decorations. Serve with cream.

Iced Fruit Salad.

Mrs. R. A. Fletcher.

Cut off top of large melon, cut inside into bits, add bananas, pines, apricots, apples and crystallized cherries cut up small. Two handfuls of sugar, and a tumbler of Kirsch or old wine. Mix and put in the melon. Replace top and ice it.

German Tart.

Mrs. P. Fletcher.

4 tablespoons flour
2 oz. sugar
1 oz. butter
Baking powder

Mix stiff with a little milk. Spread in jam-sandwich tins and bake in hot oven. When done spread with jam and serve with custard or wine sauce.

German Puffs.

Mrs. Wilson.

½ teacup of flour

2 oz. of butter or lard

1 gill (or a little more) of milk and water

1 or 2 eggs

Put milk, water and butter into saucepan, let them boil, stir in flour quickly while milk boils, stir over fire until the batter is quite smooth; remove from fire. Beat up eggs and stir them into batter. Butter some small pudding cups, half fill with batter and bake in a hot oven 20 minutes. When done serve quickly with jam or syrup.

German Pudding.

Mrs. Sly.

3 tablespoons ground rice

1 lemon

3 oz. castor sugar

3 eggs

Have some fruit cooked and cold (cherries are very nice), put into a pie dish. Beat up the yolks and sugar well together, then add the ground rice and grated rind of lemon, lastly add the stiffly-beaten whites of eggs to the mixture. Put on top of the fruit and bake in a hot oven for half-an-hour.

Ginger-Bread Pudding.

Mrs. Vintcent.

½ lb. flour

¼ lb suet

1 egg

1 teaspoon ginger

½ teaspoon soda

2 tablespoons treacle

Mix well to a batter with a little milk and boil for 2 hours.

Jelly.

Mrs. Vintcent.

To 1 quart packet of gelatine add 1 cup of cold water and leave it
to dissolve. Then add 1 cup of boiling water, 6 tablespoons
brown sugar, 1 cup sherry, 1 wine-glass brandy, 1 wine-glass
Van der Hum, 1 small stick of cinnamon, the juice of 3 lemons,
the rind of 2 lemons cut very thin, 3 cloves, 3 cardamom seeds.
Beat the whites of 2 eggs to a stiff froth, put it in with the egg
shells. Let it all boil up and then pour in half a cup of cold water.
Do this twice, then remove to one side of the stove and let it
gently simmer for half-an-hour. Then strain through a jelly-bag.

A Simple Jelly.

Mrs. LeFeuvre.

1 packet of Nelson's gelatine soaked in a cup of cold water for an
hour. Put it on the fire with a cup of hot water and when boiling
add 1 cup of white sugar and essence of lemon. When that boils
add the beaten whites of 2 eggs and set to cool. Make a custard
with the yolks of the eggs to serve with it.

Lemon Creams.

Mrs. Selmes.

Take one pound sugar, put to it half-a-pint water, the juice of 6
lemons, 1 yolk of egg well beaten, and the whites of 6 eggs
beaten to a stiff froth. Strain all this mixture through a hair sieve,
set it on the fire to thicken but not boil, stirring all the time. This
quantity will fill 12 jelly glasses. Always pare finely 3 or 4 of the
lemons, and let the peel remain in the water some little time
before adding the other ingredients.

A Spanish Sweet.

(To use the yolks left from the above).
Mrs. Selmes.

Take the yolks of 5 eggs, beat thoroughly till quite stiff, pour into small patty pans and bake in a moderate oven till slightly brown. Make a good clear syrup flavoured with lemon or vanilla, into which, while hot, throw the little cakes. Serve cold.

Baked Lemon Pudding.

Mrs. Sly.

2 lemons
2 oz. cake crumbs
3 oz. castor sugar
3 eggs
1 gill milk

Cream the sugar and yolks of eggs together until thick and white. Add the juice of the lemons, the rinds grated, the milk, cake crumbs, and lastly the whites of eggs, stiffly whisked. Have ready a pie dish with the edge lined with puff paste, pour in the above preparation and bake in a moderate oven for half-an-hour.

An Economical Lemon Sponge.

Mrs Nash.

1 packet Moir's jelly
3 tablespoons of sweet condensed milk.

Mix jelly in ordinary way but with half-a-pint of boiling water. Stand aside and when on point of cooling stir in condensed milk, whip up with an egg whisk until it becomes of a spongy consistency when it can be poured into a wet mould and is ready for use when cold.

Lemon Sago.

Mrs. Puzey.

Put 1 teacup of sago into 3 teacups of water, add the juice of 3 and rind grated of 2 lemons and 5 tablespoons of brown sugar. Boil till clear and thick, put into a mould and when cold cover

with a pint of custard and serve, or this is very nice eaten hot
without the custard.

Lemon Soufflé.

Mrs. Nanson.

Put 8 oz. of castor sugar into a basin with the grated rind of a
lemon and the yolks of 2 eggs, stir the eggs and sugar together
and pour in the strained juice of 2 small lemons, place the basin
in a stew pan of boiling water on the stove, and patiently whisk
the contents until they are the colour and thickness of boiled
custard. Have ready a quarter of an ounce of isinglass, dissolved
in a little boiled milk, stir this into the soufflé mixture, and
directly it is cool, add lightly half-a-pint of stiffly-whipped
cream and the whites of the eggs whisked to a very stiff froth.
Directly the soufflé shows signs of setting, pour into a soufflé
mould, and then, just before sending it to table, scatter some
very finely-chopped pistachio nuts or almonds over the surface.

Orange And Lemon Trifle.

Mrs. Puzey.

Squeeze the juice of 2 oranges and 2 lemons into a basin, add a
quarter-pint of cold water and 2 oz. sugar. Pour this over 4 small
sponge-cakes in a deep glass dish and when the cakes are well-
soaked pour 1 pint of thick custard on the top (cold) and
decorate with blanched almonds.

Marguerite Pudding.

Mrs Puzey.

¼ lb. flour
2 oz. butter
2 oz. white sugar
1 teaspoon of baking powder
1 egg
1½ tablespoons of milk
Flavouring of vanilla

Rub butter into flour, then add sugar and baking powder and moisten with the egg and milk. Previously grease a mould and put three or four tablespoonfuls of jam or marmalade at the bottom and then the mixture on top, cover with a greased paper and steam 1 hour.

Marmalade Pudding.

Mrs. J. Macdonald
4 oz. breadcrumbs
4 oz. suet
3 oz. sugar
2 eggs (or none)
Two tablespoonfuls of marmalade
Steam 3 hours.

Magdala Puddings.

Mrs. H. B. Thomas.
2 oz. flour
2 oz. butter
2 oz. sugar
2 eggs
½ pint milk
Preserve
Cream butter, stir in sugar and flour, add well-beaten eggs, then milk. Bake in six saucers, slightly greased, for quarter-hour. Turn out and fold, placing preserve in centre.

Nottingham Pudding.

Mrs. Issels.
6 large apples
2 oz. sugar
1 pint batter

For Artistic and Reliable Furniture—
ELLENBOGEN & CO., Bulawayo.

Write for our Illustrated Catalogue, Post Free, Box 323.

Peel the apples and take out core, fill up with sugar, place them in a pie dish, cover then with the light batter. Bake 1 hour.

Plum Pudding.

Mrs. Duncan.

1 lb. beef suet
1 lb currants
1 lb sultanas
1 lb sugar
½ lb flour
½ lb breadcrumbs
½ lb raisins
½ lb muscatels
½ lb mixed peel
6 or 8 eggs
4 oz. almonds
2 oz. butter
2 oz. citron peel
Rind of 2 lemons
¼ pint milk
¼ pint brandy
1 teaspoonful salt
1 nutmeg
Boil steadily for eight hours.

Orange Pudding.

Mrs. C. M. Parry.

For the pudding:
3 oz butter
3 oz. castor sugar
2 eggs
¼ lb, flour
½ teacup baking powder

For the filling mixture:
3 oz. castor sugar

Juice of ½ lemon
Rind of 2 oranges, the juice of 3
2 large teaspoons cornflour
¼ pint cold water
Grate the rind of 2 oranges on to the sugar, and strain on to it the juice of the 3 oranges and half a lemon. Mix the cornflour smoothly with the water, put these into a small saucepan with the sugar, &c., and let them boil for 2 or 3 minutes. Then turn the mixture into a basin to cool. Meanwhile make the pudding.

Cream together the butter and sugar, beat up the eggs and add them. Grate the rind of the orange on to the flour and baking powder, than add these to the butter mixture. Slightly butter 3 plates or shallow round tins, put a third of the mixture into each and bake in a quick oven a delicate brown. Let these cool, then lay one of the cakes on a dish, spread on it half the filling mixture, over that another cake, the rest of the filling and lastly the third cake. Sprinkle a few chopped pistachio nuts and a little castor sugar over and it is ready to serve. It may be served hot or cold.

Lemon Water Ice.

Mrs. Heyman.
Rind and juice of 6 lemons.
6 oz. of sugar.
1 pint of boiling water.
Peel the lemons as thinly as possible, put the peel into a basin with the sugar and, water, allow it to stand until quite cold, take out the peel, add the lemon juice, then freeze. Serve in mould glasses or in a rough pile.

Pumpkin Fritters.

Mrs. Vintcent.
To 6 tablespoons of sweet pumpkin boiled soft and mashed, add 4 tablespoons of flour, half egg spoon of salt, half egg spoon baking powder, and 1 egg put in last. All to be well beaten, and

fried in boiling fat. Serve with sugar and powdered cinnamon sprinkled over.

Richmond Pudding.

Mrs. J. Macdonald.

Line mould with figs, fill up with custard of three or four eggs and biscuit or bread crumbs. Steam three hours.

Railway Pudding.

Mrs. LeFeuvre.

½ lb flour
1 tablespoon butter
½ pint milk
1 teaspoon sugar
1 egg
1 teaspoon carbonate soda
1 small teaspoon tartaric acid

Mix soda and acid with flour well. Beat butter and sugar to a cream and mix with flour. Beat egg and add it to the milk and other ingredients. Pour into large buttered tin and bake 20 minutes. Cut in half and spread with jam.

Rum Omelet.

Mrs. R. A. Fletcher.

5 eggs broken in a basin, flavour with salt spoon of vanilla
Half lemon peel, free of pith, chopped
1 oz. castor sugar
3 tablespoons thick cream.

Mix well with a fork until mixture runs smooth. Then pour into a hot omelet pan in which has been melted an oz. of butter or lard. Cook over a quick fire until mixture begins to set. Then form the omelet into desired shape, leaving it somewhat moist in centre. Turn it on a hot dish, mask it over with the caramel (as below) and just when about to serve pour on the dish some best run, set it alight and serve.

Caramel. Put into a saucepan quarter lb. cane sugar, 1 wineglass rum, 2 tablespoons strained lemon juice, 2 oz. water, and a few drops of carmine. Boil until a nice golden colour. Use.

Sponge Fritters (made in a few minutes.)

Mrs. Puzey.

1 teacup of flour

¼ teacup of sugar,

1½ teaspoons of baking powder

1 egg and a little milk

Make these into a stiff batter and fry in boiling fat till a golden brown, this is done in a few seconds; when cooked put a little heap of jam on the top of each and serve hot. This quantity makes 6 good-sized fritters.

Soda Pudding.

Mrs. P. Fletcher.

3 cups flour

1 cup raisins

1 cup sugar

1 teaspoon ground ginger

Half-cup butter

Half-cup dripping

1 teaspoon soda

1 egg

One-and-half cups lukewarm water

Mix all together and moisten with egg and water. Boil 2 hours.

Tipsy Cake.

Mrs. Sly.

12 Small sponge cakes,

Raisin wine

Half-lb. jam

1 pint custard.

Soak the sponge cakes in a little of the wine, arrange them in a deep glass dish in 4 layers, putting a layer of jam between each and pour round them a pint of custard, decorating the top with cut preserved fruit. Time: 2 hours to soak the cakes.

Venetian Pudding.

Mrs. Tonge.

Make a custard with 3 eggs and a pint of milk, dissolving in the milk whilst boiling half oz. of isinglass, add a gill of cream, sweeten to taste; let it cool and begin to set slightly, then pour into a buttered mould, arranging in it some glacé cherries and some small pieces of candied peel, angelica, preserved ginger or any kind of preserved fruit may be used. If the pudding is desired richer make rather less of the custard and put in more cream.

Yankee Pudding.

Mrs. R. A. Fletcher.

2 cups of bread crumbs
1 cup of flour
3 eggs
3 tablespoons of jam
1 pinch of salt
1 dessertspoon soda

Take a cup of boiling water, into half of which melt 3 tablespoons of butter. Into the other half mix the dessertspoon of soda. Mix together and then add the other ingredients. Tie up in a floured cloth, boil and serve with custard.

Savouries.

Boules d'Or.

Mrs. Wilson.

Boil 2 eggs for 20 minutes, strip off the shells, and rub through wire sieve. Add half teaspoon grated lemon rind, 1 tablespoon finely mashed potato, a pinch of pepper and salt, a teaspoon of tomato ketchup and sufficient milk to make into a stiff paste Roll into balls and fry in boiling fat until brown.

Crème de Fromage.

Mrs. Murray.

2 tablespoons parmesan
1 oz. vermicelli
2 tablespoons cream
Cayenne and salt
1 egg
A little thin puff paste

Mix the grated cheese, cream, cayenne and salt, into a smooth thick paste, spread it over some thin rounds of puff paste, double over and press the edges well together, dip in egg and crushed vermicelli, fry in boiling fat and serve very hot.

Celery Cream.

Mrs. Swanson.

6 cheese biscuits
2 to 3 tablespoons thick cream
1½ tablespoons finely chopped celery
1 tablespoon grated cheese
Salt and cayenne to taste

Whip up cream, add celery, cheese and salt, pile roughly on to biscuits, then garnish with the tiny celery leaves and red pepper.

H. Hepker

Charter Butchery.

Contractor to the Matabeleland Civil Service
Co-operative Society.

Prime Local Beef,
Finest Colonial Mutton,
Dairy-fed Pork,
Specially Selected Poultry.

The finest quality obtainable of—
FRESH and CURED FISH,
BUTTER (local and imported)
HAMS, BACON, &c., &c., - -
always kept in stock. - - -

French and German Polonies, Cambridge
Sausages, Brawn, &c., from our own factory.

Telephone 29. *Tele. Add.* "*Hepker.*" *P.O. Box 567.*

Bulawayo.

If plain biscuits are used, double the amount of grated cheese in the mixture. Sufficient for 6 people. (Mixture should be put on biscuits just before serving).

Cheese Savoury.

Mrs. Geo. Johnson.

Cut some tolerably thick slices of stale bread into small rounds, dip them in milk and let them get thoroughly saturated. Melt a little butter and pour over them, and a few dabs of mustard. Add some grated cheese and a pinch of cayenne pepper. Place on a sheet of buttered paper and bake for quarter-hour. Do not let them get too crisp.

Cheese Soufflé.

Mrs. P. Fletcher.

3 oz. grated cheese
1 oz. flour
1 oz. butter
3 eggs
Barely a pint milk
Cayenne, salt.

Melt the butter in a stew pan, stir in the flour, add milk, and boil well. Then mix in over the fire, the yolks of eggs, beat well, then stir in the cheese and add the pepper and salt. Whisk whites to a stiff froth, add them lightly to the rest of the ingredients, pour the preparation into the soufflé, tin and bake in a hot oven 25 or 30 minutes. Serve in the tin in which it is baked and send to table quickly.

Cheese Straws.

Mrs. Vintcent.

5 oz. flour
4 oz. cheese
1 oz. butter

Quarter-egg spoon baking powder

A pinch of salt added to the flour, cayenne to taste.

Moisten with a little milk, mix lightly, then roll out and cut in strips. Bake in a quick oven.

Egg and Cream Savoury.

Mrs. Selmes

Mix with half-pint milk, 1 tablespoon flour, a piece of butter the size of a walnut. Heat this until it becomes thick, then add the whites of 4 hard-boiled eggs chopped (not too finely), add a gill of cream, pepper, salt and cayenne. Pour the whole into a well-buttered dish, grate the yolks of the 4 hardboiled eggs over it, with a little chopped parsley, and brown it slightly in the oven.

Eggs *au Gratin*.

Mrs. Venning.

2 hard-boiled eggs

¾ oz. butter

¾ oz. flour

1 teacup milk

2 tablespoons grated cheese

2 tablespoons browned crumbs

Pepper, salt and cayenne

Make a sauce with butter, flour and milk, season it and put a small quantity in a pie dish. Slice the eggs and lay some on the sauce, then sprinkle with cheese. Repeat the layers and sprinkle the last with crumbs. Bake five minutes.

French Rolls.

Mrs. Tonge.

Quarter-pint of water

1 oz. of butter

2 tablespoons of flour

2 oz. cheese, grated fine

3 eggs

Pepper, salt, mustard

Boil the water and butter, then add the flour, stirring well till well cooked, then add pepper, salt, mustard and the eggs, one at a time; let it get cool and fry drops of the mixture in boiling fat.

Ham Toast.

Mrs. Heyman.

Some rounds buttered toast
2 eggs
Quarter lb. lean boiled ham
1 tablespoon cream
Cayenne pepper
Half oz. butter
Half teaspoon minced parsley

Break the eggs into a saucepan, add all the ingredients and stir over gentle heat until it begins to set. Pile on the rounds of toast. Dish on a lace paper resting each round on the other. Garnish with parsley and serve.

Mayonnaise and Egg Savoury.

Divide some medium-sized tomatoes in half and remove all the seeds and hard portions. Cut the latter in small pieces and put it into a basin with some cucumber cut into small dice, and some finely shred crisp lettuce, and mix the whole with mayonnaise. Fill the halves of the tomatoes with this mixture and stand the hard-boiled yolk of an egg upright in the centre of each. Serve on a bed of lettuce or watercress.

Potato and Cheese Savoury.

Mrs. Brooks.

Mash half lb. of boiled potatoes with 1 oz. butter, 1 tablespoon milk, a dash of cayenne pepper and 3 oz. grated cheese. Put into small greased ramekin cases and bake a light brown in hot oven.

Sweet Potato Chestnuts.

Mrs. Chataway

Parboil some sweet potatoes for 5 to 10, minutes, peel them and cut into pieces about the size and shape of chestnuts. Put them into an enamelled saucepan with just sufficient water to cover them, and about a teaspoon of sugar, and boil until quite tender. Then drain and put them in a hot vegetable or entree dish. Put the yolk of an egg into a saucepan, add a teaspoon of sugar, half a teacup of strong coffee, and a tablespoon of cream or milk, stir, and when boiling pour over the chestnuts and serve very hot.

A Simple Savoury.

Mrs. Clarkson Fletcher.

Boil one large onion till quite tender. Remove outside skin, chop very fine with fork or wooden spoon and add a piece of butter the size of a large walnut and 2 oz. of grated cheese. Pile on rounds of toast and serve very hot.

Tomato Toast.

Mrs. Heyman.

Half-lb. of tomatoes

2 eggs

2 oz. butter

1 dust of sugar

1 teaspoonful vinegar

Some rounds or squares of toast.

Pepper, salt, cayenne

Slice the tomatoes and fry in butter five minutes, rub through a sieve, put pulp back into the pan, add eggs (not beaten), seasoning, sugar and vinegar, stir until it begins to set. Butter toast and put on the mixture (piled up). Garnish with parsley or cress.

A Good Savoury from Stale Cheese.

Miss Hodges.

Grate the cheese to a fine powder and mix with it a little cayenne. Whip the white of an egg to a stiff froth, beat the cheese in lightly (one white will take almost an ounce of cheese) and drop teaspoonfuls into boiling fat. Drain on soft paper and serve at once.

A Dainty Savoury.

Mrs. P. G. Hunt.

Take 4 cold hard-boiled eggs, shell and cut in half, cut a little piece off each end so that they may stand. Take out the yolks and pound in a mortar, with a little butter and enough anchovy sauce or paste (or Liebig) to flavour the eggs, with cayenne to taste. Spread some small rounds of toast with butter and place on each a cup formed of the half egg, filling them with the mixture of the yoke and anchovy paste. Arrange them in a circle on a dish, with cheese straws piled tip in the centre. Garnish with parsley.

Things to Remember.

A dash of salt added to the whites of eggs makes them whip better.

Add a teaspoonful of water to an egg used for crumbing in order to remove the stringiness.

A pinch of bi-carbonate of soda mixed with tomato before milk or cream is added prevents the milk from curdling.

Milk and butter should be kept in closely-covered vessels, as they readily absorb flavour and odour from other articles.

Crumbs to spread over the tops of dishes should be mixed evenly with melted butter over the fire; this is a better method than having lumps of butter dotted over the crumbs after they are spread.

Meat should not be washed, but rubbed with a damp cloth.

Dishes which are to be frozen need an extra amount of sweetening.

Flour raisins before adding them to a mixture in order to prevent their settling at the bottom.

Breakfast, Luncheon and Supper Dishes.

A Good Porridge.
Mrs. Ll. Webb.
2 small breakfast cups of flour,
1 egg,
Half-quart of milk
Pinch of salt.
Beat the egg in a little milk and mix the flour, egg, milk and salt into a batter, roll out and cut into fine strips. Put the half-quart of milk on to boil, and when boiling put the strips of paste in and cook for one and a half hours slowly.

American Salad.
Mrs. Nanson.
Cut some new potatoes, young carrots, beetroot and celery (all previously cooked and thoroughly drained) into slices and then into rounds rather larger than a shilling, and cut up some slices of smoked tongue sausage, also in rounds, and a few slices of apple. Make an ordinary mayonnaise dressing, dress the vegetables with the mixture and arrange them in a salad bowl. Then put an edging of mustard and cress or finely shredded lettuce and some crossed strips of filleted anchovy on the top, and lastly, sprinkle some finely-minced parsley over the whole.

Babotee—A nice way of doing up cold meat.
Mrs. Glanville.
Mince cold meat, doing with it a little bread and an onion; moisten well with milk. Mix and add 1 tablespoon curry powder, 1 tablespoon sugar, 2 tablespoons vinegar. When whole is thoroughly mixed, place in pie dish and pour over top an egg beaten up with a little milk (or cold potatoes seasoned and mixed with milk). Bake until warmed well through and brown on top. Rice to be eaten with this, as with curry.

Brawn (Beef).

Mrs. Brooks.

3 lbs. shin of beef
12 peppercorns
12 cloves
3 or 4 blades of mace
1 teaspoon salt
1 nutmeg grated

Put the shin (bone and all) into a saucepan of water. The meat must be more than covered with water. Add the salt and let this boil for about 8 hours, or until the meat leaves the bones cleanly. Remove all the bones and cut the meat into small pieces. Put the cut meat back into the saucepan with all the spices and the liquor the shin was boiled in, and let it simmer 1 hour. Pour into moulds or basins and put in a cool place to set.

Breakfast for One.

Mrs. C. M. Parry.

2 eggs well-beaten
Half breakfast cup of milk
½ cup sifted breadcrumbs
A little salt

When the eggs are well beaten, add the other ingredients and mix lightly together. Put a little butter in an omelette pan and, when very hot, pour in the mixture. Let the pan remain for a few minutes over a clear fire. Brown on the top in a very hot oven or before a bright fire. An onion (previously cooked) chopped fine, may be added, if liked, or some mixed herbs.

Chicken Pasty.

Choose a plump young fowl and boil until tender, adding to the water in which it was boiled a little thyme and 1 small onion. When done, skin the chicken, remove the meat from the bones, and cut into small pieces. Strain the liquor and add salt and pepper to taste. Line a baking dish with a piece of good short crust. Have ready three hardboiled eggs, and put them between

Wreford and Matthews

GENERAL DRAPERS

P.O. Box 102, BULAWAYO.

WE CATER FOR YOU!

And invite your special attention to our extensive stocks of all that is New and Seasonable. Latest Novelties arriving weekly from Best British and Continental makers, including

MILLINERY, BLOUSES. COSTUMES,
DRESS SKIRTS. JACKETS. DUST COATS,
DRESSING GOWNS, ETC.

A Big Range always on hand of—

LADIES' AND CHILDREN'S UNDERCLOTHING,
BABY LINEN, DRESS MATERIALS, SILKS,
LACES, RIBBONS, FANCY GOODS.
HABERDASHERY AND HOUSEHOLD DRAPERY.

Civility and Attention a Password.

Country Orders Receive our Personal Attention

SAVE TIME AND MONEY BY PURCHASING AT

Wreford and Matthews

layers of the chicken inside the crust. Pour the liquor and one tablespoon of cream over, and then cover with a crust. Brush over the top with beaten egg, and cut three long gashes to allow the steam to escape. Bake in a moderate oven until brown. This is a particularly nice supper dish, and is delicious eaten hot or cold. If preferred cold, add to the liquor while hot 1 tablespoon of gelatine dissolved in a very little water.

Children's Dinner Dish.
Mrs. Norman Chataway.
Grease a baking dish and line the bottom with slices of bread spread with dripping, over this put a layer of raw meat cut in pieces and dipped in a mixture of salt, pepper and any seasoning liked, over this place a layer of scalded onions in slices, and repeat these layers until the dish is full, having bread as the top layer, spread on the upper side with dripping. Pour over enough stock (water may be used but stock is nicer) to thoroughly soak the bread, cover the dish and bake in a moderate oven for an hour or until the meat is done. Uncover the dish for the last quarter or half hour in order that the surface may get nicely browned and crisp. Cooked rice or macaroni may be substituted for part of the onion.

Durham Cutlets.
Mrs. LeFeuvre.
6 oz. cold minced meat
6 oz. bread crumbs
1 teaspoon salt and a little pepper
1 tablespoon mushroom ketchup
One-third cup stock or gravy
One and half oz. butter
One and half oz. flour
Half teaspoon curry powder
Put the butter and flour into a saucepan and when dissolved add stock, curry powder, salt, pepper and ketchup. Let this simmer for 3 or 4 minutes and then add minced meat and 3 oz. bread crumbs; mix thoroughly and set aside to cool. Shape into cutlets,

using macaroni as bones. Dip in egg and breadcrumbs and fry to a light brown.

Fish Kedgeree.
Mrs. Heyman.
Boil some rice well and see the grains are separate. Put in a saucepan with some butter; break up any cold fish into small pieces, and hard-boiled eggs (chopped). Add pepper, salt and half a teaspoon of curry powder, stir it well and serve very hot. A nice breakfast dish.

Hot Pot (To do up cold meat).
Mrs. Vintcent.
Take a pudding basin, put in a layer of raw sliced potato, then a layer of cold meat, a layer of onion and a little pepper and salt. Repeat this until the basin is full. Take a breakfast cup of stock or any gravy, mix with teaspoon of flour and pour into the basin. Put into the oven and cook for 2 hours. Serve in basin.

Minced Ox Kidney on Toast.
Mrs. Granger.
Put the kidney through the mincing machine, then put into a saucepan with 2 oz. of butter, and allow to simmer until cooked, stirring all the time. Add a little chopped parsley. a little cayenne and salt, and 2 eggs (which have been well beaten). Stir over the fire for 10 minutes and serve on hot toast. This is a nice breakfast dish.

Meat Roll.
Mrs. Issels.
Take 1 lb. beef-steak, half lb. ham, a small nutmeg grated, half pound of bread crumbs. Mix well together (as if kneading bread) with one or two eggs, and pepper and little salt. The beef and ham must be put through the mincing machine twice to get rid

of all the skin. Make into a roll like a roly-pudding, tie in a cloth and gently boil for 3 hours. Glaze and serve cold.

[A quick and economical glaze is made by dissolving half oz. of gelatine to half pint of water and stirring in a teaspoon of extract of meat and a few drops of liquid browning. Apply to the roll with a soft brush. Ed.]

Mince Pie.

Mrs. Selmes.

Chop very finely or pass through a mincing machine the remains of any cold meat and 2 cold potatoes. Add the juice and soft pulp of 2 large tomatoes, salt, pepper and moisten very thoroughly with some good stock. Well grease a pie-dish and sprinkle thickly with breadcrumbs. Put in the mince and cover with breadcrumbs. Put small pieces of butter or dripping on the top and bake till the crumbs are brown and crisp.

Scalloped Mutton and Tomatoes.

Mrs. Naake.

Cut up some cold mutton and a few tomatoes which have been peeled. Crumb 2 slices of bread. Put a layer of crumbs at the bottom of a baking dish then one of mutton, and then one of tomatoes. Season each with salt, pepper and bits of butter. Let the top layer be of tomatoes with a sprinkle of bread crumbs. Bake three quarters of an hour and serve hot.

Grand Hotel,

Bulawayo.

HOTEL DE LUXE.

PATRONISED BY THE ELITE.

The Finest and most Up-to-date Hotel in South Africa.

80 Bedrooms.

Private and Public Drawing and Sitting Rooms.

First-class Cuisine.   Terms Moderate

Hot, Cold and Shower Baths.

Tennis Courts and Garden adjoins the Hotel.

T. McMurray, Lessee

Potato Puffs.

Mrs. Ll. Webb.

Select 6 medium-sized potatoes of as nearly as possible the same shape. Scrub thoroughly and put in the oven in their skins to bake. When done cut a round rather larger than a shilling from the tops of the potatoes, and with a vegetable scoop remove the inside taking care not to break the skins, mash the inside well with butter, pepper, salt and 1 egg, then lightly fill the hollow skins with the mashed potato, and bake in oven until nice and brown.

Potato Salad.

Mrs. Glanville.

Boil potatoes in their jackets. SAUCE: beat up 3 eggs with vinegar and a little salt; let the mixture boil. When cool, add milk (whipping well to prevent curdling) till it is of proper consistency. Slice the potatoes and lay them in layers sprinkled with a little salt, pepper and chopped onion, and pour sauce over each layer.

Tomato and Mutton Stew.

Mrs. Crake.

Cut up 2 lbs. ribs of mutton and an onion, let it stew in a flat saucepan for an hour, then add 8 or 10 tomatoes cut in slices, with a teaspoon of salt, a pinch of sugar, and half a red chili. If there is a great deal of liquid, remove the lid and let it simmer till it is all a rich creamy-looking sauce. Remove any fat. Serve very hot with plain boiled rice.

Scotch Eggs.

Mrs. Vintcent.

3 eggs, 3 sausages, breadcrumbs. Boil the eggs hard, then roll the contents of a sausage round each egg, smoothing the mince on

with a wet palette knife, then egg and bread crumb. Cut in half and fry in boiling fat. Serve with tomato sauce very hot.

Tomato Sauce (for the above).
4 lbs. tomatoes
1 large onion
1 oz. of butter
1 gill of water
Cook until tender, then strain.

Vegetarian Brawn.

Mrs. Norman Chataway.
1 lb. macaroni
2 oz. maizena
Half-lb. tomatoes
6 hard-boiled eggs
2 oz. grated cheese
2 raw eggs
1 teaspoon sage and parsley mixed
1 tablespoon mushroom ketchup (or curry paste if preferred.
Salt, pepper and half-pint water.
Boil the macaroni, cut into half-inch lengths, and put in a saucepan. Pour half-pint of boiling water over the tomatoes and sieve them, leaving skins and pips behind. Add with the water to the saucepan, chop fine a large cooked onion and add it with the grated cheese and other seasonings, and stir till it boils. Mix in the maizena dissolved in a little water and boil for a few minutes, stirring well. Take from the fire and add the beaten raw eggs gradually, beating hard, and lastly, the hard-boiled eggs in slices or dice. Fill a mould and set on ice or in a cool place until quite stiff. Turn out and garnish with lettuce or parsley.

Bread, Cakes and Biscuits.

Bread.

Mrs. Winslow.

Take 2 breakfast cups of water that potatoes have been boiled in, 1 tablespoon flour, 1 tablespoon sugar, and half dessertspoon salt. Mix these into the potato water when cool and bottle in a well-stoppered bottle. This should have risen sufficiently in 24 hours for use. Take 1 breakfast-cup of this yeast, 2 breakfast-cups warm water (the warmth of new milk) and into this beat about 2 breakfast-cups of flour until it is a fairly thick batter. Cover and leave to rise for about 2 hours when it should look light and spongy. Into this batter knead the flour for bread, make into loaves, and set to rise in the bread tins. Bake in a hot oven. Always start fresh yeast with some of the old left in the bottle.

Boer Meal Biscuits.

Mrs. Norman Chataway.

4 oz. Boer meal
2 oz. flour
One and half oz. butter
One and half oz. sugar
1 egg
Half tablespoon golden syrup
Half teaspoon baking powder

Rub the butter into the meal and flour and add the baking powder and sugar. Make a hole in the centre and break in the egg and pour in the syrup, then mix the whole thoroughly together. Roll the paste out very thin, prick over with a fork, stamp out with a tin cutter any size or shape preferred and bake in a brisk oven until crisp.

Fairy Biscuits.

Mrs. P. Fletcher.
5 cups flour,
2 sugar
1 butter
3 eggs, if necessary a little milk
Baking powder.
Rub the flour, powder and butter together. Beat the eggs and
sugar. Mix well. Roll and cut into shapes. Currants may be
added if liked.

Plain Rusks.

Mrs. C. M. Parry.
1 lb flour
3 oz. butter
1 egg
Quarter pint new milk
2 teaspoons baking-powder
Mix the baking powder and flour and rub in the butter. Beat the
egg, add the milk, and mix with the dry ingredients. Roll out to
about quarter inch in thickness and cut into rounds. Bake in a
hot oven for about 10 minutes. When a nice pale biscuit colour
take them out and split each with a knife. Put into the oven again
for a few minutes, split side up, till they are nice and crisp. To
sweeten add 2 teaspoons sifted sugar.

Plain Fruit Loaf.

Mrs. Norman Chataway.
1 lb. flour
6 oz. stoned raisins
6 oz. butter
6 oz. sultanas
Half pint milk

2 eggs

Half teaspoon bicarbonate of soda

Rub butter and flour together, add the fruit. Beat up eggs with the milk and stir in the soda. Mix all well together quickly, turn in to a well-greased bread tin, and bake in a quick oven for 1¼ hours.

Albert Cake

Miss B. L. Fynn.

¾ lb. of flour

6 oz. sugar

Quarter-lb. butter

1 egg and the yolks of four more

1 teacup sultana raisins

Half-teacup mixed peel

1 teaspoon baking powder

2 cups milk

A little essence of lemon

Beat the butter and eggs until foamy, add the sugar, beat well again. Pour in the milk and flavouring. Sift together the flour and baking powder and add to it the fruit. Pour in the liquid and beat again. Turn the mixture into a large shallow tin and bake in a hot oven (or make two cakes, using smaller moulds).

Bachelor Cake.

Mrs. J. Macdonald.

Beat 1 lb. sugar with quarter-lb. butter for 15 minutes, add 1 lb. raisins, 1 oz. mixed spices, 2 oz. orange peel, one-and-a-half tbs. of flour. Mix 3 teaspoons of carbonate of soda, 1 teaspoon tartaric acid with 3 teacups of butter-mill: and bake in a moderate oven for two hours. (If no butter-milk, fresh will do).

Banana Cake.

Mrs. R. A. Fletcher.

1¾ cups flour
Half-breakfast cup butter
Half-breakfast cup milk
2 eggs
1 cup sugar
1 level teaspoon baking powder
Cream butter, add sugar gradually, then beaten yolks of eggs;
add sifted flour with the baking powder alternately with the
milk, and lastly, stiff whites. Bake in two flat cake tins. Put
banana filling between and cover top with icing sugar, mixed to
a smooth paste with lemon juice and water.

Banana filling for above
Remove the skin and coarse threads of enough bananas to fill a
cup, pass through a sieve, add one cup sugar, juice and rind of
one lemon, and the unbeaten white of one egg. Beat with a
perforated wooden spoon until solid to the bottom of bowl. This
will take about 20 minutes. Then spread between the cake layers.
This filling may also be served in glasses, or used as a filling for
Charlotte Russe.

A Very Good Brown Cake — No Eggs.
Mrs. R. H. Myburgh.
1 lb. flour
Half-lb. butter (or butter and fat mixed)
Half-lb. currants
Half-lb. sugar
Half-lb. raisins
2 tablespoons vinegar
2 teaspoons bicarbonate of soda
1 teaspoon cream of tartar
Mix with milk, mixing all dry ingredients first, except the
bicarbonate of soda, which add last of all with the vinegar. Bake
slowly.

Chocolate Cakes (Iced).

Mrs. Glanville. 4 oz. flour
3 oz. butter
3 oz. sugar
3 oz. grated chocolate
3 eggs
1 teaspoon baking powder
10 drops lemon or vanilla essence

Mix cream, butter and sugar together, add chocolate and flour (sifted) mixed, alternately with well-beaten eggs to creamed butter and sugar. When well mixed add essence and baking powder. Place in buttered patty pans and into hot oven. Cakes to be iced when cool.

Icing

Half lb. icing sugar, put through sieve, one and half oz. grated chocolate, 1 teaspoon flavouring essence, 1 tablespoon water (about). Mix essence and water with chocolate and stand the basin in hot water. Add the sugar, mix well, dip cakes into icing and stand on plate in cool oven or before the fire to glaze.

Cocoanut Cakes.

Mrs. G. A. Pingstone.
2 cups cocoanut
2 tablespoons flour
1 cup sifted sugar
White of 2 eggs

Well beat the eggs, then add sugar, cocoanut and flour. Oven must not be too quick.

Cocoanut Cones.

Mrs. Ingham.
Quarter-lb. white sugar
2 oz. grated cocoanut

The whites of 2 eggs.

Beat the whites of the eggs with a pinch of salt to a stiff froth. Stir in lightly the cocoanut and sugar with a wooden spoon. Have ready a plank of wood the size of your oven, cover with small squares of paper about 3-in. square, put a tablespoon of the mixture in each square of paper, shape into a cone, and bake in a moderate oven till a light brown, or to feel firm to the touch. Slip each cake off the paper with a knife and put back in the oven on the board, to dry at the bottom.

Drop Scones.

Mrs. Byers.

1 breakfast cup flour

1 dessertspoon baking powder

2 tablespoons sugar

1 egg (may be omitted)

Milk to make a fairly thick batter.

Mix flour, sugar, and baking powder together, add the milk, to which a well-beaten egg has been added, and beat the mixture thoroughly. Put a pan on fire with some good beef dripping in it; when hot, drop in the batter, a spoonful for each scone. When cooked on one side, turn and allow to get light brown; drain on paper. Good, hot or cold, with butter.

French Wafers.

Mrs. I. R. B. Baxter.

Half-oz. butter

2 oz. sugar

2 oz. flour

One-and-a-half teacups milk

2 eggs

Beat the butter and sugar to a cream; beat the eggs well and add then, beating them thoroughly in; stir in the flour smoothly, and, lastly, add milk by degrees; beat well. Butter some round Yorkshire pudding tins, and put a thin layer of the above batter in each; it should be sufficient for six. If more convenient, flat saucers may be buttered and used. Bake in the oven for to or 12 minutes. Serve on a hot dish, one on the top of the other, with lemon curd between, or castor sugar only, if preferred. Then, with a sharp knife, cut across into four, as they are more convenient to serve thus.

Filbert Cake.

Mrs. Byers.
1 lb. flour
4 eggs
Quarter-lb. castor sugar
6 oz. filberts
2 oz. butter
Pinch of salt
Beat the yolks of the eggs with the blanched and pounded filberts (or almonds may be used) and sugar. Add the flour, into which has been mixed the butter and salt. Whip the whites of the eggs to a stiff froth, and add to the mixture, beating all the time. Bake in a well-buttered cake tin in a moderate oven, turn out and, when cool, ice with the following: the white of one egg worked with icing sugar, on which the 4th part of an orange has been rubbed, until of the consistency of thick cream, then mask the cake with it.

Fruit Cake (without eggs).

Mrs. Vintcent.
Half-lb. flour
Quarter-lb. butter
Quarter-lb. raisins
Quarter-lb. castor sugar
Quarter-lb. currants
Half-breakfast cup milk.
4 oz. candied peel
1 teaspoon mixed spice

Half-teaspoon soda. Mix well and bake in a moderate oven for 2½ hours.

Genoa Cake.

Mrs. Sly.
10 oz. flour
8 oz. butter
8 oz. sugar
6 oz. sultanas
3 oz. candied peel
2 oz. almonds
4 eggs
1 teaspoon baking powder
Grated lemon rind
Cream the butter and sugar, add all the dry ingredients mixed and the eggs alternately. Bake 1½ hours in moderate oven.

Very Cheap Ginger Loaf.

Miss Hendrie.
Melt a teacupful of butter and mix it with the same quantity of treacle, slightly warmed, a teacup of sugar, a teaspoon of ground ginger, and 2 teaspoons of cinnamon. Beat together ten minutes, dissolve 2 large teaspoons of carbonate of soda in a cup of cold water. Stir it into the mixture and add enough flour (3 cups) to form a stiff batter. Stir again for a few minutes and bake in a moderate oven.

Ginger Bread.

Mrs. Duncan.
Three-quarters lb. flour
10 oz. golden syrup
Quarter lb. sugar
Quarter lb. butter
2 oz. candied peel

Bulawayo Public Library.

THE Library comprises about 7,000 volumes in all classes of literature and the latest works are added monthly as funds permit.

The Reading Room contains all the chief Home and Colonial Papers and Magazines, and is free to all residents and visitors.

HOURS—Reading Room, 9.30 a.m. to 10 p.m. every day throughout the year. Books are issued on Mondays, Wednesdays and Fridays from 10.30 a.m. to 1 p.m. and 2 p.m. to 6.30 p.m. ; Tuesdays and Thursdays from 10.30 a.m. to 1 p.m. and 2 p.m. to 5.30 p.m.; Saturdays from 10.30 a.m. to 2 p.m. Books are not issued on Sundays or Public Holidays.

SUBSCRIPTIONS Full Privileges £2 per annum, payable yearly, half-yearly or quarterly in advance, and a deposit of 10/- from all subscribers. Monthly tickets 5/-

Reading Room. Free.

The Board Room may be obtained for meetings at a small charge.

Further information may be obtained from

P.O. Box 218. D. NIVEN, Librarian.

2 eggs
4 tablespoons milk
2 teaspoons ground ginger
Half teaspoon soda
Mix flour, salt, ginger and peel together. Melt syrup, butter and sugar and pour hot over the flour. Beat the eggs, mix the soda in the milk, and mix all together. Bake in a flat baking tin lined with buttered paper, in a cool oven.

Hard Times Cakes.

Mrs. R. M. Townsend.
1 lb. flour
6 oz. dripping, lard or butter
Half lb. sugar
2 oz. candied peel
1 breakfast-cup of currants or raisins
Half pint milk
1 teaspoon bicarbonate of soda
Mix dry ingredients together with butter and milk, keeping back a little milk to dissolve the soda lastly. Butter must previously be whipped to a cream. The milk and butter must be added together. The soda, etc., must be thoroughly stirred into the mixture, or cake will be streaky. Bake in a moderate oven. This cake is improved by the addition of one or two eggs if they are plentiful.

Jumbles.

Mrs. Franklin White.
Take 3 eggs
1 cup sugar
½ cup butter
Flour to thicken
3 tablespoons milk
2 teaspoons baking powder
1 teaspoon nutmeg.

F. E. WOODS,

𝔅aker and Confectioner,

Abercorn Street and Ninth Avenue.

Box 573.   Telegrams " FEW."   'Phone 138.

Best White, Brown and Malt Bread.

All the Latest Novelties in Confectionery for Afternoon Tea - - Parties, Receptions, etc. - -

Brides', Birthday and Christening Cakes.

Only the very best ingredients used in all the above, and satisfaction guaranteed.

Vans deliver to all parts of the Town and Suburbs.

Cream butter and sugar together, and add in their order the beaten eggs, and baking powder, nutmeg and flour. Sprinkle granulated sugar over the sheet of cake dough and pass the rolling-pin over. Cut out and bake.

Kisses.

Mrs. Puzey.
Half-breakfast cup sugar (castor)
Half-breakfast cup flour
Not quite quarter-lb. butter
1 breakfast cup cornflour
1 egg
1 teaspoon baking powder
Beat butter and sugar to a cream, then add the egg the flour and cornflour by degrees, and, lastly, the baking powder. Put small pieces on to a flat tin and bake in a hot oven. When cold, put a little apricot jam on one and place another on top to make a sandwich.

Lord Zetland Cake.

Mrs. Issels.
Half lb. sugar, three-quarters lb. butter. Beat these well together and add 6 eggs beaten, three-quarters lb. flour, quarter lb. lemon peel, half-lb. currants, half lb. sultana raisins, quarter lb. almonds. Bake nearly 4 hours.

Old Testament Cake.

G. A. Pingstone, Esq.

			Chap.	Verse
4½ cups of	1 Kings		4	22
2	"	Jeremiah	6	20
2	"	Nahum	3	12
2	"	1 Samuel	30	12
2	"	Numbers	17	8

Bulawayo Board of Executors and Trust Company, Limited.

CAPITAL - £15,000.

Directors:

C. P. J. COGHLAN, ESQ. *(Chairman).*

COL. H. M. HEYMAN, M.L.C.   CAPT. W. B. BUCKNALL.

COL. W. NAPIER, C.M.G.   A. H. ANSTEE, ESQ.

AGENTS FOR—

> The Union-Castle Mail S.S. Co., Ltd.
> Sun Insurance Office.
> Guardian Assurance Co., Ltd., of London.
> Commercial Union Assurance Co., Ltd.
> Northern Assurance Company.
> Union Assurance Co., Ltd. (Life).
> Rhodesia Hotels Co., Ltd.
> Rock Life Assurance Company.

The Company undertakes.—The Administration of Estates as Executors, Administrators, Trustees and Liquidators ; The Management of Affairs of Residents and Non Residents ; The Lending of Money ; The Sale and Purchase of Landed and other Properties ; Secretaryships of Companies and Tributors ; Accountancy and Auditing in all its branches.

R. M. DUNCAN, Secretary.

P.O. Box 26.   Tel. Address: "EXECUTORS."

12	"	Judges	4	19
Half lb. of		Judges	5	25
6		Jeremiah	17	11
2 teaspoons of Amos			4	5
A pinch of Genesis			19	26
Season to taste with 2 Chron.			9	9
Directions in Proverbs			23	14

Bake one and a half to two hours.

Oven Scones.

Miss Hendrie.

Half lb. flour, or a little more
2 oz. butter (or tablespoon dripping)
1 salt spoon salt
1 oz. sugar
2 large teaspoons baking powder.
Mix together with sweet milk; brush over with egg. Put out very soft and bake in a quick oven.

Orange Cake.

Mrs. R. M. Townsend

The weight of 2 eggs in flour, castor sugar and butter. Deduct a little of the sugar. Cream the butter and remainder of sugar together. Beat the whites and yolks of eggs separately, add rind of one orange (if not too big) and juice of half. Paper and butter tin well. Bake in moderate oven; when cold, ice with icing sugar and remainder of orange juice (strained). Is best kept for a day or two before cutting.

Plain Cake Mixture

Mrs. Swanson.

To each egg take 1 level tablespoon butter, one and a half tablespoons sugar, 4 tablespoons flour, about half teaspoon baking powder, a little salt, few raisins if liked, and about 2

Wightman & Co.

LIMITED.

Produce and General Merchants,

BULAWAYO AND SALISBURY.

Large Stocks of Produce always on hand.

Wankie Coal and Firewood stocked.

Try our special Mixed Grain for Fowl Feeding, also Oyster Shell Grit.

MOLASSINE MEAL, the best "Patent" Food for all Horses, Cattle, Sheep, &c.

Crushed Oats for Horse Feeding always on hand.

Enquiries for all lines of produce solicited.

tablespoons or rather more of milk or water. Beat butter and sugar to a cream, add eggs well-beaten, then milk or water, lastly, flour (sifted carefully with baking powder). It should be of the consistency of thick batter. Bake in well-greased tins, either small or large.

Plum Cake.

Mrs. J. Macdonald.

1 lb. currants
Half lb. flour
6 oz. fresh butter
6 oz. soft brown sugar
Quarter lb. orange peel
2 oz. treacle (black)
1 oz. sweet almonds
3 fresh eggs
Quarter pint warm milk

Beat butter, sugar and treacle to a cream, add one egg at a time, beating well, then add the warm milk, then the fruit and, lastly and lightly, the flour. Don't make batter too soft.

Scotch Shortbread.

Mrs. J. Macdonald.

1 lb. flour
Quarter lb. butter
Quarter lb. lard
Quarter lb. sugar

Rub butter and sugar all together, then work in the flour, roll out into thin cakes, nick edge with finger and thumb, prick top all over with fork and bake in moderate oven until a light brown.

Shortbread.

Mrs. Crake

4 oz. flour

2 oz. butter

1 oz. castor sugar

Mix all in a basin, roll with tips of fingers till it binds well, roll out on a floured board, and cut in shapes. Decorate with sweets or candied peel and bake in a slow oven for 20 or 30 minutes. Dredge well with sugar before and after baking.

Seed Cake.

Mrs. R. A. Fletcher.

1 lb. fine flour, 3 oz. *crème de riz*. Rub this through sieve and put it to warm. Work in 1 lb. of butter until smooth and white. 1 pinch cinnamon, 1 large pinch grated nutmeg, 2 oz. caraway seeds. Work into this a lb. castor sugar, and add by degrees raw yolks of 9 eggs and quarter oz. of baking powder. Work all together for 10 or 12 minutes, then add the whites of 9 eggs beaten to stiff froth, with pinch of salt. Add this to the mixture of flour and other ingredients. Paper and brush the cake moulds over with warm butter. Pour in the mixture and bake in a moderate oven for one hour. This quantity is sufficient for 3 medium-sized cakes, and if the paper is left on and they are put in a tin, they will keep well.

Lemon Jelly Cake.

Mrs. Venning.

The weight of 3 eggs in butter and sugar, quarter lb. flour, 1 teaspoon of baking powder. Cream the butter and sugar, add the eggs unbeaten one by one alternately with the flour, beat all well together, spread on 3 small plates and bake in a moderate oven.

Jelly.

Three-quarters cup of water, three-quarters cup of sugar. Put into a saucepan. Grate in 2 lemons and add the juice of 1. Let it boil and stir in a well-blended tablespoon of arrowroot. Set at the side of the fire till clear, and when cool spread on two of the cakes.

Nice Tea Cake.

Mrs. R. M. Townsend
2 breakfast cups flour
¾ breakfast cup of sugar
1 tablespoon butter
1 breakfast cup milk
3 teaspoons baking powder
1 or 2 eggs
Essence of lemon, candied peel or grated orange
Mix the dry ingredients together first and then rub in the butter, and add milk and eggs lastly. Bake in a moderate oxen. To be eaten hot or cold, with or without butter.

Raspberry Buns.

Mrs. Uttley.
Mix 6 oz. of ground rice, and same of flour. Rub in quarter lb. lard, same of sugar, and a teaspoon of baking powder. Mix into a stiff paste with the yolk of an egg and a little milk. Divide into balls, hollow each and insert a little jam. Close up and dip in white of egg. Bake in a sharp oven.

A Novel Sponge Cake.

Mrs. Venning.
Boil 5 oz. castor sugar with half gill water. Beat up 3 eggs, pour the boiling sugar gradually on to them, whisking all the time, and continue to whisk for 20 minutes. Stir in 4 oz. sifted flour with some grated lemon rind in it, pour into a greased and-papered tin and bake in a moderate oven 30 minutes.

THE
Standard Fruit Store

Wholesale and Retail,

EIGHTH AVENUE (Opposite the STANDARD BANK),

Always holding the Largest and Best Variety of Fruit
and Vegetables in town.

Vegetables direct from the Farm Daily and supplied
at the Lowest Possible Prices.

Watercress supplied in Large and Small Quantities.

—— FRESH EGGS A SPECIALITY. ——

All Orders attended to Promptly and with Civility.
We solicit a Trial Order.

Our Motto is " Small Profits and Quick Returns."

P.O. Box 27.).   Tele. Address : " :IYATT," Bulawayo.

Sponge Cake.

Mrs. Vintcent.

Six eggs, their weight in sugar, half their weight in flour. Beat the yolks and sugar well together, then add the whites beaten to a stiff froth; lastly, dredge in the flour, add a small pinch of baking powder, and flavour with lemon essence. Bake in a moderate oven for three-quarters of an hour.

Sultana Cake.

Mrs. Wickwar.

Three-quarter lb. flour
8 oz. butter
6 oz. sugar
6 oz. sultanas
4 eggs
2 small teaspoons baking powder
A few chopped almonds if liked
Flavouring to taste.

Beat butter and sugar to a cream, then add the eggs (well-beaten) alternately with the flour and sultanas. Mix all well together and bake in a moderate oven for about 1 hour. Sufficient for 2 cakes.

Victoria Sandwich.

Mrs. Uttley.

4 oz. butter
4 oz. sugar
4 oz. flour
2 eggs
A small teaspoon baking powder

Beat butter and sugar to a cream, add eggs well-beaten, then flour, and mix well. Baking powder last.

Filling for Sandwich Cakes.

Mrs. Byers.

For a moderate-size cake, 1 tablespoon butter and enough icing sugar well beaten together to a thick cream, then flavoured with vanilla. A few chopped walnuts added is a great improvement.

For Making Jam Sandwich Roll.

Mrs. P. G. Hunt.

A successful way of getting a sponge roll to roll is by adding cream of tartar and carbonate of soda to the other ingredients when it will be found that the cake will roll up like a piece of flannel. One teaspoon of cream of tartar and half a teaspoon of carbonate of soda to about 2 cups of flour.

Sandwiches.

Curried Almond Sandwiches

Mrs. Heyman.

Fry some onion in butter or dripping, make a paste of curry, mixing it with vinegar or lemon, sugar or jam of any kind, a little Worcester sauce, and some stock and cream. Blanch and chop the almonds and add to the curry paste. It is then ready for the sandwiches. The same will keep for several days.

Sardine and Olive Sandwiches.

Miss Hodges,

Take as many sardines as you think you will want and allow to each sardine one large olive. Remove skins and bones from sardines and stones from olives, and pass them both through the mincing machine. Then work together with a sufficient quantity of butter to make a nice paste, add a sprinkling of cayenne or paprika and, if liked, a dash of tarragon vinegar. This mixture is very good with brown bread.

Various Fillings For Sandwiches.

I. Chopped chicken and celery mixed with mayonnaise.
2. Chopped lobster mixed with mayonnaise and laid between lettuce leaves on the bread and butter.
3. Chopped olives, grated cheese and mustard,
4. Mock crab, 1 tablespoon butter, 2 tablespoons grated cheese, 1 salt spoon each of salt, paprika and dry mustard, a little anchovy paste, and 1 teaspoon vinegar, all rubbed to a smooth paste, and spread between thin slices of dry toast.
5, Chopped walnuts, cream and a little sugar.
6, Hard-boiled eggs chopped fine and mixed with a little highly-seasoned white sauce, and the bread spread with butter mixed with chopped parsley.
7. Herring or cod's roe mixed with mayonnaise.

Pickles and Preserves.

Recipe for Canning Fruit.

Mrs. P. Fletcher.

For 3 lbs. peaches make a syrup of 2 cups sugar and 4 water, boil
up and add the peaches. Boil until the peaches are tender (a
good way to test them is with a straw). Put the fruit into bottles,
fill with the syrup and screw down the cover at once. Pears do
not require much sugar, apricots and quinces rather more. The
sugar is merely a matter of taste and does not make the fruit
keep any better. The great secret of success in canning fruit is to
have the bottles hot and fill them up and screw down as quickly
as possible, and keep tightening them as they cool. Be careful not
to stand the hot bottles in a draught or on a damp table or they
will crack.

Inexpensive Apricot Jam.

Mrs. Nash.

Well wash 2 pounds of dried apricots and pour on to them 4
quarts of boiling water. Cover and leave for 48 hours. Then
simmer gently till the fruit is tender—probably about an hour
and a quarter—add 7 lbs. of sugar, boil again for an hour, put
into pots and cover down at once.

Preserve (Green Apricot).

Mrs. Hull.

100 green apricots, and their weight in sugar. Prick the fruit with
a steel pin, lay them in a deep dish, sprinkle some salt over them
(about a dessertspoon), pour boiling water over, cover with
green vine leaves—this keeps them green—lay a plate on the
top. Now proceed to make the syrup, taking a cup of water to a
cup of sugar. When it is boiled and clarified, take the apricots
out of the salt water wash them and pour the boiling syrup over

them. Leave for a night. The next day preserve by gently simmering till the fruit is nice and clear.

Chutney.

Mrs. Crake.
2 lbs. chopped apples
1 oz. raisins stoned and chopped
1 large onion chopped finely
½ lb. moist sugar
Half-oz. ground ginger
½ oz. cayenne
Pinch of salt,
1 pint of vinegar.
Boil all together for 1 hour, well mashed and stirred at times.

Chutney (Blatgang).

Mrs. Duncan.
1 lb. dried apricots
Half-lb. brown sugar
Half-lb. almonds
Quarter lb. fresh chillies
Quarter-lb. salt
12 large onions
1 garlic
2 bottles vinegar
2 tablespoons crushed coriander seeds
Soak the apricots in vinegar over night. Put the chillies through the mincing machine twice, after removing the seeds. Remove the outer skins of the onions and bake them in the oven on an enamelled dish and pass them through a mincing machine, also the apricots and almonds. Boil all these ingredients till nice and clear, stirring all the time. Bottle and cork well.

Chutney.

Mrs. Hall and Mrs. P Fletcher.

3 lbs. of apricot or quince jam, 2 tablespoons finely pounded chillies, 1 breakfast-cup of finely-chopped shallots, 10 drops essence of lemon. Stir in enough English vinegar until consistency required.

Green Fig Konfyt.

Miss. B. L. Fynn.

Peel the figs carefully, make 4 slits in each, put them into an earthen jar, sprinkle a handful of salt over them, press them down with a plate, pour boiling water over them and let them stand for 12 hours. Take them out and put them on to boil in fresh water. When they are soft, take them and squeeze them well. Prepare the syrup, allowing 7 lbs. sugar to 100 figs; water, half-pint to each lb. of sugar. Put in the figs when the syrup thickens and boil gently. When the figs are first boiled they become yellow, but when then are put into the syrup they soon regain their green colour. A small piece of alum may be put to the water in which they are soaked.

Lemon Essence.

Mrs. R. B. Baxter.

Fill a bottle with rectified spirit, and, when using lemons, cut off the yellow part of the rind and place in the spirit. You will find this quite as good as the essence of lemon sold in the shops. Essence of orange can be made in the same way.

Lemon Cheese.

Mrs. H. B. Thomas.

3 eggs

Half lb. sugar

2 oz. butter

One and a half lemons (grated rind and juice)

McCullagh & x Whitehead

BULAWAYO.

| VALUE | The Three Centres - Round which - |

Specialists in Ladies' and Gentlemen's

CONSISTENCY

Our Business Has Grown.

Wearing Apparel, Boots and Shoes.

ORIGINALITY

Our Buyers supply us weekly with Novelties as they are produced.

x

McCULLAGH & WHITEHEAD

Beat all together and then stir in a jug (stood in a saucepan of boiling water) until it is the consistency of honey.

Lemon Mincemeat.

Mrs. C. M. Parry.
3 large or 4 small lemons
1 lb. beef suet
1 lb. moist sugar
1 lb. currants
Quarter lb. candied peel
Quarter lb. sponge cake
Quarter lb. sweet almonds
Quarter pint brandy
Quarter pint sherry
Finely chop the beef suet and candied peel, blanch and chop the almonds, and crumb the cake. Peel the lemons, then squeeze out the juice. Boil the peel till quite tender and let it drain all night. Next day beat it up to a paste, add the suet, sugar, currants, mix all together with the lemon juice and add peel, cake, almonds, and lastly the brandy and sherry. Stir well till thoroughly mixed, put into a jar, press a piece of white paper over the mincemeat and then tie down the jar. If wanted for use at Christmas, it should be made early in November, as it is much improved by keeping.

Orange Marmalade.

Mrs. Hull.
Cut the oranges into quarters, remove the pulp and pips and cut the peel into shreds according to taste. Weigh the fruit and peel and to each lb. of this add 3 pints of cold water; let this stand 24 hours. Boil gently till tender, let it stand another 24 hours, then boil again and to every lb. of fruit add three-quarters lb. of loaf sugar. Boil and stir, not too fast, for about 1 hour till the colour darkens slightly and it begins to thicken. Try a little on a plate to

cool, and if it jellies it is finished. Pour into jars and let it stand till next day before tying down. About 4 oranges go to the lb.

Mealie Pickle.

Mrs. Norman Chataway.

10 mealies cut from the cobs, 2 onions, 1 green pepper, half red pepper, a small head of white cabbage, all chopped finely, half cup salt, half cup flour, 2 small cups sugar, 1 tablespoon ground mustard, 1 tablespoon celery seed, 2 tablespoons mustard seed, Half tablespoon turmeric powder. Mix mealies and chopped ingredients with 3 pints good wine vinegar and let all come to a boil. Mix flour, turmeric, sugar, salt, mustard and seeds into 1 pint vinegar, pour over pickle, boil for 30 minutes, bottle while hot. In about 10 days ready for use.

Naartje Konfyt.

Miss B. L. Fynn.

Pare the naartjes very thinly, cut 4 slits in each, soak them in water, changing the water every day for two days and squeezing each naartje to get out the pips, boil and drain them well. Make the syrup allowing 1 lb. of sugar to each lb. of fruit weighed after they have been boiled; half pint of water to each lb. of sugar. When the syrup begins to thicken, put in the naartjes and boil gently till quite clear.

Pickled Quinces or Pears.

Mrs. Geo. Johnson.

To 18 lbs. of fruit put 9 lbs. of sugar and one and a half pints of vinegar and 1 oz. cloves. Wipe quinces with a cloth, but do not peel them; quarter and core and let them stand in the vinegar and sugar all night. In the morning let them boil till soft, but do not let them mash up. Put in jars and when cool tie down like jam.

Rosella Jelly (An old Queensland recipe).

Mrs. Granger.

Put the rosellas into a preserving pan with a little water to every pint of fruit. Allow it to boil for 2 or 3 hours, then strain through a sieve. Put 1 lb. of sugar to every pint of juice, and put this back into the preserving pan and boil for 1 hour or until it jellies in a saucer. When cool fill preserve jars and do not fasten up until cold.

(Rosellas are not very commonly grown here in Rhodesia, but will grow quite easily in sandy soil.. They deserve to be better known. Ed.)

Ripe Tomato Jam.

Mrs. Clement Dixon.

4 lbs. ripe tomatoes
4 lbs. sugar
4 lemons
Half-pint water

Boil sugar and water for 5 minutes, add tomatoes (peeled in boiling water) sliced thickly, and lemons peeled and cut up finely. Boil up quickly and skim. Will take about one-and-half hours.

Tomato Chutney.

Mrs. Norman Chataway.

4 lbs. ripe tomatoes
1 lb. apples
Half-doz. small onions
4 oz. salt
1 oz. mustard
½ oz. grated ginger
1 salt spoon cayenne
1½ pts. best malt vinegar
Sugar in proportion to the fruit—about 1 lb.

' Blue Brand '
Aerated Water Factory.

TO HOUSEWIVES.

Should you at any time be doubtful as to the absolute purity of your drinking water, you cannot do better than obtain a supply of the Blue Brand Mineral Waters, about the purity of which there can be no possible doubt.

Mr. G. A. PINGSTONE. F.C.S., Analyst to the Bulawayo Municipal Council, has visited the Blue Brand Aerated Water Factory and has reported on his inspection as follows :

" I have visited the " Blue Brand " Aerated Water Factory and find the following system of Sterilization and Manufacture now in force :

The water is pumped direct from a deep well (bricked in cement and coated with the same material from top to bottom) to a storage tank ; from this— by gravity—it passes to a huge copper cauldron of 800 gallons' capacity, where it is sterilized by being raised to boiling point, and kept so for about half-an-hour. This serves the double purpose of sterilization and the removal of a large amount of Lime. The Lime is then allowed to settle and the water drawn off into properly constructed covered " coolers." When cool the water is further purified from any suspended matter by mechanical filtration through a " Berkfeld " Filter, from which it passes directly to the aerating machines. The analysis of the water at this stage shows it to be an *alkaline mineral water of excellent quality*, and the composition is as follows :—

			Grains per Gallon.
Bicarbonate of Magnesia	...	...	19·13
,, ,, Lime	...	...	2·96
Silica	...	...	3·99
Oxides of Iron and Aluminium	...	...	·71
Sodium Chloride	...	...	5·03
Sulphates	...	...	Nil

The process from well to bottle is entirely mechanical, this obviating any accidental pollution after sterilization.

The water is highly charged with Carbonic Acid Gas, and from its composition compares equally with imported aerated waters.

GEO. A. PINGSTONE.

It is not necessary that your order be a large one. Small orders are delivered. Prices on application to—

BLUE BRAND AERATED WATER FACTORY.

Break the tomatoes into a preserving pan and add the apples in quarters, not peeled or cored, chop the onions and add with all the other ingredients. Boil the whole slowly to a pulp and rub through a coarse hair sieve. Add when cold 3 or 4 oz. of finely-chopped raisins. Leave for a day before bottling. This chutney improves with keeping.

Mrs. Lionel Phillips' Grape Juice.

Mrs. R. A. Fletcher.
Select a juicy variety grape (Hermitage is good, also Barbarossa). Pick from the stems, rejecting bad ones. Wash well. Put on to boil without water. Cook until grapes burst open. Turn into strong jelly bags. Drain without squeezing. Re-heat this juice and seal boiling-hot in air-tight bottles or jars. The jars or bottles must be over-flowing so that no air remains. Will keep indefinitely. When the juice is opened to be used it can be diluted with water to suit the taste. Add at least half as much water.

Pickled Green Tomatoes.

Mrs. Wickwar.
Remove the stalks from a quantity of small green tomatoes, choosing them as much of a size as possible. Put them into a colander, pour some cold water over them, shake, drain well, and then spread on a large dish. Peel and slice up half-a-dozen good sized onions, mix among tomatoes and then sprinkle the whole freely with salt. Leave until next day. Drain off resulting brine, place the vegetables in a preserving pan, add 4 oz. of Demerara sugar, 2 teaspoons each of peppercorns and allspice, 1 teaspoon of cloves to each half-peck tomatoes and enough vinegar to cover. Bring to the boil and allow to simmer gently for about 1 hour. Put in earthenware jars when quite cold and cover in the usual way.

Philpott & Collins,

Beverages

Cooling Drink for an Invalid.

A refreshing summer drink for an invalid is to add the very thinly cut rind of half a lemon and ten drops of lemon juice to two teaspoons of Plasmon tea. Pour over this one pint of boiling water. Let it stand for a few minutes, sweeten to taste, and strain. If liked cold, this is delicious put on ice before being served.

Home-Made Ginger Beer.

Mrs. P. G. Hunt.

Boil 3 oz. of bruised ginger for half an hour and have ready a 3 gallon bucket of warm water, in which should be 3 lbs. white sugar, 4 oz. Cream of Tartar, 1 breakfast cup of yeast. Add the ginger, let stand 24 hours, strain and bottle. Ready for use in about 5 days.

The 'Knock-Out.'

H. de Laessoe, Esq.

1 glass port wine
1 liqueur glass green Chartreuse
Half glass sherry
1 tablespoon absinthe
1 lump sugar
1 lump crushed ice

Lemonade.

Mrs. Clarkson Fletcher.

1 lb. lump sugar
1 oz. tartaric acid
2 large lemons

Palace Hotel

(NEXT PALACE THEATRE.)

Best and most popular Hotel in Bulawayo. Sixty large commodious bedrooms, well furnished, and lighted with electric light throughout. Bathrooms, with hot and cold water laid. Large Dining Room. Excellent Cuisine. ————Only the Best Liquors and Cigars stocked.———— Four-in-hand Coach, and 'Bus for accommodation of guests.

Palace Theatre

(NEXT PALACE HOTEL.)

One of the largest and finest theatres in South Africa. Splendid accoustic properties. Stage, 78ft. by 35ft. Capable of accommodating any Company and any Production. Proscenium Opening, 26ft. 4ins. wide, by 22ft. 6ins. high. Excellent accommodation in Dressing, Orchestra, and Storage Rooms. This Theatre is capable of seating 1,000 people. The only Theatre in Bulawayo. Terms reasonable. Apply

W. R. PATERSON,

P.O. BOX 520.   Sole Proprietor of Palace Hotel and Theatre
TELEPHONE 19.   **BULAWAYO.**

Peel the lemons very thinly and put the rind into a good pint of cold water. Let it come to the boil and simmer for 10 minutes. Put the sugar and tartaric acid into a basin with the juice from the lemons. Pour on to this the boiling liquid and stir well until the sugar is dissolved. Let it stand 24 hours, then strain and cork up tightly. 2 or 3 tablespoons to a tumbler of water or soda-water.

Mint Lemonade.

Into a large jug put quarter lb. of granulated sugar and squeeze upon it the juice of 6 lemons. When the sugar is dissolved, put into the jug half-a-dozen stalks of mint, slightly bruising some of the leaves between the thumb and finger, and add a pint of very cold water. Pour over two bottles of ginger ale and use.

Lemon Syrup.

Mrs. G. A. Pingstone.

2 lbs. sugar, 1 quart water; boil together, then, when quite cold, mix well in one and a half oz. of citric and tartaric acid, mixed in equal quantities, and 1 teaspoon essence of lemon, then strain through muslin.

Lime Juice (Excellent).

Mrs. Heyman.

9 cups of cold water
4 lbs. white sugar
1 bottle essence of lemon
3 oz. citric acid

Put citric acid, sugar and water to boil for ten minutes, let it get nearly cold, add the essence of lemon, strain through flannel and bottle. This juice added to water makes a most excellent water ice.

The Rhodesia - Trading Co., Ld.

Bulawayo.

PURVEYORS OF—

Cold Storage Produce, Ice & Liquor

AGENTS FOR—

Le Plaisir Merle Wines and Brandies.
Rennie's Aberdeen Line of direct Steamers.

HEAD OFFICE :
Finsbury Pavement House, London, E.C.

LOCAL HEAD OFFICE :—
Salisbury, Rhodesia.

BRANCHES : Beira. Umtali. Penhalanga. Hartley.
Gadzema. Victoria. Enkeldoorn. Inez.
Lomagundi. Makowries.

Roman Punch.

N. H. Chataway, Esq.

Boil 1 lb. sugar with one and a half pints of water and the strained juice of 10 lemons, then strain it and let it cool. Beat to a stiff froth the whites of 4 eggs, and mix with them half-a-bottle of pineapple rum, mix in the syrup and freeze.

Iced *Café-au-Lait.*

Add enough cold black coffee to milk to give it the desired strength and flavour, sweeten to taste and let it stand on ice till ready to serve. Any coffee left from breakfast prepared in this way makes a most refreshing drink for luncheon in hot weather.

Van Der Hum.

Mrs. R. H. Myburgh.

1 bottle good Cape Brandy
2 tablespoons finely-cut naartje peel
1 teaspoon bruised cinnamon
1 teaspoon bruised cloves

Allow all this to stand for 3 months and then strain, and mix 1 cup of very thick clear syrup with 2 good cups of the brandy. For syrup use 7 cups brown sugar to 5 cups water. Boil 3 hours or more till thick and clear. (The best naartjes are the thin-peeled ones; the less pith the better).

Tea Cup.

Mrs. Norman Chataway.

Make 1 quart of tea and pour it off the leaves. When cool sweeten it. Slice 2 lemons very thin and add; and lastly add a tumbler of brandy. Mix well in a large glass jug and put in enough ice to make it thoroughly cold.

The Zambesi Cocktail.

H. de Laessoe, Esq.

3 tablespoons London dry gin
1 tablespoon lime juice cordial
1 teaspoon Angostura bitters
Soda-water to make 1 pint, ice if procurable.

Confectionery.

Almonds, Up-To-Date
Miss Hodges.
Remove the stones from some nice plump dates, and substitute blanched almonds, then fill up the openings with a dab of icing, (Icing sugar mixed to a thick paste with hot water and used immediately will do). Spread out dates on dish till icing is hard.

Cocoanut Ice.
Mrs Clement Dixon.
4 cups of sugar
2 cups of cocoanut
1 cup of sweet milk
Boil 5 minutes, divide into two; colour one pink and beat the two mixtures till stiff, then turn on to a buttered dish and when cold cut into squares.

Cocoanut Ice.
Miss B. Jackson.
Half-pound desiccated cocoanut, one and half lbs sugar (icing sugar preferred), 1 cup milk. Carefully dissolve sugar in milk and let it boil, then add cocoanut and boil 10 minutes, turn half out into a tin lined with paper, colour the remainder with a little cochineal and pour on to the white. Cut before quite cold.

Russian Toffee.
Mrs. N. Chataway.
2 teacups white sugar
2 tablespoons golden syrup
3 oz. butter

134

1 tablespoon vinegar
1 tin condensed milk
Flavouring essence

Melt butter in saucepan, add sugar and syrup, when quite melted, add vinegar and boil a few minutes, then add milk, stirring, all the time. When sufficiently boiled, add vanilla or other flavouring, and pour into a well-buttered tin to cool.

Turkish Delight.

Mrs. Glanville.

Soak 1 oz. gelatine in half-cup of water for 2 hours. Put it into preserving pan with 1 lb. white sugar, 1 teaspoon citric acid and three-quarter cup cold water. Boil 10 minutes, then add 1 teaspoon essence of lemon. Strain mixture through muslin on to 2 dinner plates (wetted with cold water). Colour one plateful pink with couple drops cochineal, leave in cool place till firm. Cut into squares, roll in sifted sugar.

Walnut Creams.

Mrs. Norman Chataway.

1 lb. icing sugar, a tablespoon or rather more of cream, a pinch of cream of tartar, a few drops of colouring essence of any kind preferred, and a little vanilla or other flavouring. Shelled walnuts in halves. Rub the sugar through a fine sieve into a bowl, add the cream of tartar, and mix in the cream and flavouring to taste, until it is a stiff firm paste. Leave it for an hour, then turn the cream on to a marble slab or pasteboard well dusted with icing sugar and knead with the hand for a few minutes. Roll out with a rolling-pin well-sugared, using icing sugar to prevent sticking, as you would flour in cake making. Take pieces the size of a walnut, roll it between the hands into a ball, press half a shelled walnut on each side, and leave to dry on sugared tins or paper about 24 hours. Any of the cream left over may be mixed with some chopped almonds and a drop or two of almond essence, rolled out as before, cut into small squares, and left to dry and harden in the usual way.

ATKINSON & WINSLOW

BULAWAYO.

Tel. Address: "LADDER."   P.O Box 88.

STOCK AND SHARE BROKERS,
MINING AND ESTATE AGENTS
SECRETARYSHIPS UNDERTAKEN.

Secretaries —

**The Bulawayo Stock Exchange & Transfer
Agency, Limited.**

Agents for—

The Union-Castle Mail Steamship Co., Ltd.

North British & Mercantile Fire Insurance Co.

**South African Mutual
Life Assurance Society.**

Railway Passengers' Assurance Company
(Accident, Employers' Liability, and Fidelity Guarantee).

Walnut Toffee.

Mrs. Brooks.

1 lb. white sugar

1 teaspoon golden syrup

Half cup Ideal milk and half-cup water mixed

Boil this together till it makes a soft ball when dropped in cold water, It must not be hard. Remove from the fire and stir in 4 oz of chopped walnuts. Beat with a fork till nearly cold, then add 1 teaspoon vanilla. Turn into a buttered till, and when cool cut into squares

Invalid Dishes.

Hydropathic Pudding.

Miss Henderson.

Remove the crust from a rather stale loaf and cut very thin slices from it. Butter a basin and line it with the bread. Have some stewed fruit cooked with sugar (currants, raspberries, etc.) and put a few spoonfuls in the basin, cover with a layer of bread then more fruit, and so on till the dish is quite full. Place a plate on top with a heavy weight, and let it stand till next day when it will turn out.

A more delicate pudding can be made by substituting sponge cake for bread.

Mock Omelette.

Mrs. N. Chataway.

Take a saucer that will fit over a saucepan of boiling water, and rub it with a little butter. Set it over the pan to heat while the yolk of an egg is beaten with a tablespoon of milk, the white of the egg beaten to a stiff froth being added last, with, if for a savoury dish, a pinch of salt and pepper and a sprinkling of chopped parsley, or, if for a sweet dish, a little sugar. Pour into the saucer, put a second saucer or the saucepan lid over the top and cook for 5 or 10 minutes until set.

Nutritious Coffee.

Mrs. Carbutt.

1 tablespoon coffee, 1 cup of water freshly boiled. Heat the coffee can first. Use boiling milk with the coffee and add sugar

W. B. RAMSAY,

Hardware Merchant,

Corner of Abercorn St. and Selborne Av.

❀❀❀❀

DIRECT IMPORTER OF

Builders' Ironmongery, Tools.

Paints, Oils, Glass, &c., &c.

P.O. BOX 258.   TELEPHONE 118.

There are MAXIMS here.
There are MAXIMS there.
There were MAXIMS firing everywhere;
But if you want the MAXIM Fare,
Enquire at the MAXIM, Market Square.

J. JAMES,
Proprietor.

according to taste. Then beat up an egg and add the coffee a little at a time to the egg. Stir well and serve hot.

Rusk Pudding.

2 or 3 finger rusks
1 gill of warm milk
1 egg
Crumble the rusks into a buttered half-pint basin, beat the egg and milk together and pour over, leave for a little while to soak, then tie a paper over and steam for 20 minutes. This is nice hot or cold, and may be served with jam, syrup, or stewed fruit.

Tapioca Cream.

Miss Henderson.

Take 2 small tablespoons of tapioca and soak in cold water till quite clear. Put in a pan with a pint of milk and sugar to taste. When thoroughly cooked draw the pan to the side of the fire and stir in the yolks of 2 eggs. Remove the pan from the fire and stir in the whites of the eggs which have previously been whipped to a stiff froth. Add some flavouring and put in a dish till cold. Serve with stewed fruit or cream.

Vermicelli Jelly.

(Very nutritious).
Half lb. veal or lean of neck mutton
Half lb. gravy beef
1 oz. isinglass
1 oz. vermicelli
3 pints cold water
Pepper and salt
Cut the meat up very small and put in the water, bring to the boil very slowly, add the other ingredients and simmer for 4 to 5 hours, skim well from time to time, carefully strain to get rid of all fat, A little wine or brandy may be added, if ordered, after

RHODESIA MOTOR CO. TELEPHONE 108.

CHAR-A-BANC TIME-TABLE.

SUNDAY.

8.15 a.m.—To Departing Mail Train from Office. Route: 12th Avenue to Park Road, Suburbs, thence by Park Road to 6th Street, returning to Post Office via Selborne Avenue.

8.30 a.m.—Leave Post Office for Departing Mail, returning same route immediately after departure.

FARES.

Suburbs to Post Office	...	...	**1s.**
Suburbs to Station	...	...	...	**2s.**
Post Office to Station ...	...	...	**1s.**

Children under 8, Half-price.

FRIDAY.

8.30 a.m.—To Incoming Mail Train from Office. Route: 12th Avenue to Park Road, Suburbs, thence via Park Road to 6th Street, returning to Post Office via Selborne Avenue.

8.45 a.m.—Leave Post Office for Incoming Mail, returning same route immediately after arrival.

FARES.

Suburbs to Post Office	...	...	**1s.**
Suburbs to Station	...	...	...	**2s.**
Post Office to Station ...	...	...	**1s.**

Children under 8, Half-price.

All Passengers are requested to see they obtain Tickets.

—✳✳—

— **PRIVATE MOTOR CARS FOR HIRE BY DAY OR HOUR.** —

straining. If preferred cold pour it into shallow vessels and put in a cold place.

White Wine Whey.

Mrs. Carbutt.

Take half-pint of milk and boil. When boiled throw in a wine-glass of good sherry. Allow it to stand and cool in porcelain dish. The curd will separate from the whey in cooling. Then strain through muslin. 1 or 2 tablespoons at a time will be quite sufficient to take, as it is very nourishing.

J. Garlick,

Fife St.   BULAWAYO.   Box 191

Best Assortment of Kafir Truck in Rhodesia.
Green, Proofed Bucksails.
Cocoa Matting & Jute Cloth for Cyanide Works
Hand-Carts, Enamelware, &c.

R. MITCHELL & CO.,

: Wholesale and Retail :

Butchers and Purveyors

ENTERPRISE BUTCHERY, BULAWAYO.

——— P.O. Box 475. ———

Finest Quality of Fresh Beef, Colonial
Mutton, clean fed Pork, Lamb & Veal.

——— DAILY DELIVERIES. ———

Veldt Cookery.

Ducks à la Polynesia.
Major R. Gordon, D.S.O.
Put a very hot stone inside the bird; then wrap all up in banana leaves and bury in a wood fire for 20 minutes or so. Time to leave in fire much depends on the size of the fire. Feathers need not be removed till after cooking. This is optional, but if not removed till after cooking, all come away quite readily then and leave the bird quite nice and clean.

Curried Lobster.
Stir in a saucepan over the fire 1 cup hot water, 1 tablespoon butter, 1 tablespoon flour, 1 teaspoon curry powder, pepper and salt and 1 cup milk. When it boils, add the meat from a tin of lobster, cut up small, let it simmer two or three minutes, and serve very hot.

Dop Flame-Pudding.
Cut up a tinned sponge cake in neat pieces and arrange on a tin dish, saturate with good Cape Dop just before serving, pour some round and set it alight, Serve while blazing.

Johnnie Cakes à la Queensland.
Major R. Gordon, D.S.O.
To every pannikin of flour (1 lb.) add 1 teaspoon of Eno's fruit salt, mix with water or milk, and make into round cakes, say about half-inch thick, and 3 inches in diameter. Coat well with dry flour before placing them on hot wood coals or wood ash to cook. The ash will then be easily removed when the cakes are cooked.

When using the Recipes in this Book,
it is necessary to have the Best Quality
of Goods, therefore for your

BEEF, MUTTON, LAMB, PORK, FISH, HAMS, BACON, BUTTER, POULTRY, ETC.,

GO TO ——⊂ဝ

MALEVRIS BROS.

Market Place.

Telephone No. 117.   ———   P.O. Box 568

(Contractors to B.S.A. Co , and the Memorial Hospital.)

146

Mealie Meal Fritters.

Sprinkle mealie meal into salted boiling water until stiff, stirring all the time. Spread out on a flat dish to cool, then cut into strips, roll in flour and fry in boiling fat.

'Sudden Death.'

With Liver-Lemon Sauce.

N. H. Chataway, Esq.

Put a pan of cold water on the fire, chop the head off a fowl, and hang up, neck downwards, until the water boils. Then draw it and plunge it in the boiling water, when the feathers and skin will come off quite easily. Split the fowl in half, lay it on a gridiron over a clear fire and keep turning frequently until done, which will take from 15 to 20 minutes. Pepper slightly at each turn, and salt at the last turn. Rub over with butter and serve very hot with liver-lemon sauce, which make as follows: throw the liver of the fowl into boiling water and let boil for 5 minutes, then take out and chop small. Put a tablespoon of butter into a small saucepan, when melted, stir in a tablespoon flour and, when bubbling, a cup cold water, and stir until it thickens, then add the chopped liver and the juice of a lemon or a little lemon essence, stir for a minute longer and serve.

Veldt Pie.

Cut into small pieces some beef or game, put a layer of these with pepper and salt in a billy can, over this a layer of sliced onion, and over this some sliced raw potatoes, repeat until the billy is half-full or more. Then put in water up to the last row of potato, and cover the whole with a lid of paste made with beef suet or dripping, flour and baking powder, mixed with cold water to a stiff paste. Put on the lid of the billy, stand it in a pot of boiling water and boil for one and a half to two hours.

148

Miscellaneous.

Boot, Floor and Furniture Polish.

Mrs. J. R. B. Baxter.

1 lb. beeswax

Five and half pints cold water

2 pints turpentine

3 oz. bicarbonate of potash

Put beeswax, potash and water on slow fire in saucepan to melt. Stir now and then. When melted pour into a dish and add turpentine. Must be stirred continually till cool, then bottle.

Furniture Polish.

Mrs. Vintcent.

1 tablespoon vinegar,

1 tablespoon salad oil

1 tablespoon turpentine

The yolk of an egg .

Put in a bottle and shake well.

Stain for Floors.

N. H. Chataway, Esq.

Mix about a gallon of new linseed oil with umber about the size of an egg, the quantity of umber according to shade required. Add half that quantity of patent drier, which can be bought at any oil shop. This stain penetrates the boards and will not wear off.

Stain For Floors.

Mrs. Franklin White.

1 gallon raw linseed oil, half-lb. burnt umber (powder), 3 lbs. burnt sienna powder. When quite dry polish with beeswax and turpentine.

Homely Remedy for Burns And Scalds.

Mrs. Norman Chataway.

Make a strong solution in water of either washing soda or Epsom salts. The salts are the best application for the face, head or neck. Dip soft clean cloths in the solution and apply to the burns, and keep constantly wet with the solution. This gives instant relief from pain, and will effect a complete cure if the cloths are kept constantly wet.

Remedy for Flies.

Mrs. P. G. Hunt.

Clusters of cloves hung up in a room and allowed to dry will drive away flies better than fly papers. Mignonette is also a good thing.

Cleaning Blinds.

Mrs. Issels.

This is a great stumbling block in many households, for washing blinds never really answers, they get so hopelessly out of shape. I have found it best to take them down, lay on a large clean table, and rub with bath brick, both as a brick and in powder. This is a most satisfactory way of cleaning blinds.

A Novel Cushion.

Mrs. Nash.

An eiderdown, when not in use, makes a capital and comfortable cushion if carefully folded and put into a pretty chintz or silk slip.

Mint Sauce From Dried Mint.

Mrs. P. G. Hunt.

In making mint sauce from dried mint, pour the vinegar boiling hot on the mint. It will be found a great improvement.

S. H. Baldwin,

Stock and Share Broker
and Financial Agent,

I, Willoughby's Buildings, Bulawayo.

Tel. Address: "ESAITCH."   P.O. Box 75.

G. M. Isaac,

Stockbroker, Mining and
Financial Agent,

5, Agency Chambers, Bulawayo.

Postal Add.—Box 524.   Tel. Add.: "VIVENE."

Head Office for Rhodesia of—
The Equitable Life Assurance Society of United States

For Preserving Colours in Washing.

Mrs. Tonge.

For keeping the colours of pale blue or mauve in washing, use 1 tablespoon vinegar to each quart of water. For yellow, 1 tablespoon methylated spirit to each quart of water. For black, white or grey, salt in the same proportion, also in the rinsing water. Salt and vinegar can be used together.

For Taking Out Stains.

Mrs. Tonge.

1 oz. spirits of ether rubbed on will take out oil stains. Boiling milk will take out ink stains.

To Restore Furniture Badly Smeared.

Mrs. Nash.

Slightly moisten a soft cloth with paraffin and wipe all over the article to be polished, not using too much paraffin, and leave for an hour or so, then take a clean soft duster and rub dry. Finish with usual polish.

Three Useful Hints.

Mrs. Granger.

1. A couple of sheets of big newspaper wrapped about ice will keep it half as long again as ice that is uncovered. The paper is much more cleanly than a piece of blanket, as it can be removed daily.
2. To prevent linen from fading, put a little borax in the water and let it stand for 1 hour.
3. St. John's Liniment. The yolk of an egg, 1 wineglass vinegar, 1 wineglass spirits of turpentine. Rub in for sprains, rheumatism or swellings.

154

Hints for Camping Out on Cold Nights.

H. de Laessoe, Esq.

Remember that the cold comes from below as well as from above. To keep warm it is not sufficient to pile blankets on top. An equal number should be used to lie on. Sleeping on a stretcher is very much colder than sleeping on the ground. When using a stretcher either a cork mattress or a waterproof sheet should be spread over it to keep the draught away. Paper, being fairly wind-proof, will answer in an emergency. If the night is windy at all, great comfort and additional warmth will be derived from making a wind-break of branches, a spare waterproof sheet, or, if available, cases and other camp furniture. Always sleep with your feet towards the direction from which the wind comes. It will be found much warmer. A tent is but cold comfort and it will be found much warmer to sleep in the open by a good fire. If, however, a tent is used considerable comfort may be derived from placing in it two or three large stones which have previously been heated in the fire for a couple of hours.

To Make a Housekeeper.

Mrs. Taylor.

Take equal quantities of economy, industry, regularity and cleanliness. Let them boil moderately together in an old-fashioned vessel called a conscience. When cool add a little spirit of authority and good humour to your taste. Cleanse your vessel well before you put in the ingredients, and dip the cover in a little essence of watchfulness, which will prevent them from separating. If not clear put in a few grains of resolution, which will make it bright. It will be fit for use in two or three years, and will keep a long time and be better for age. Be very careful in following the directions of this recipe and it will never fail.

The Rhodesia Medal Roll
David Saffery (ed.)

Containing the names of 12,000 medal recipients, and revealing nearly 2,000 previously unpublished decorations, this definitive book is the ultimate compendium of Rhodesian military and civilian honours and awards gazetted between 1970 and 1981. Fully indexed by surname, it is perfect for medal collectors and dealers, historians and genealogists—and a brilliant heirloom souvenir for recipients and their families.
ISBN: 0-9553936-0-4

Where the Lion Roars: An 1890 African Colonial Cookbook
Mrs. A. R. Barnes

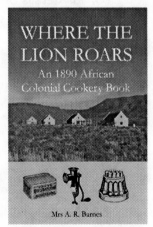

A reprint of one of Africa's very earliest and scarcest English-language cookery books, dating from 1890. Mrs. Barnes' recipes for translucent, aromatic melon and ginger konfyt; fiery curries; and sweet peach chutney are as delicious now as they were a century ago; while instructions for making a canvas water cooler, and for treating snake-bite or fever, offer a fascinating insight into the domestic lives of southern Africa's Victorian colonists.
ISBN: 0-9553936-1-2

Also available from Jeppestown Press

The Anglo-African Who's Who 1907
Walter H. Wills (ed.)

A reprint of Walter Wills' quirky colonial reference book, containing the details of nearly 2,000 prominent men and women of Edwardian Africa. This astonishing work includes biographies of settlers, soldiers, explorers, politicians and traditional leaders from every corner of the continent. Invaluable for genealogists, historians, military researchers and medal enthusiasts, it offers details of over 1,200 separate medal awards, together with fascinating biographical sketches of colonial African celebrities—many of whom were known personally to the editor. ISBN: 0-9553936-3-9

For full details of our inventory, or to order direct, view our web site at **www.jeppestown.com**

JEPPESTOWN

CPSIA information can be obtained at www.ICGtesting.com
Printed in the USA
LVOW08s0844030314

375762LV00001B/227/A